Praise for *The Dark Days of Abraham Lincoln's Widow*

"The tale of Mary Lincoln's mental derangement, her incarceration in a mental hospital, her release four months later, and her subsequent estrangement from her only surviving son forms one of the saddest chapters in the Lincoln family saga. When Jason Emerson wrote his revelatory study *The Madness of Mary Lincoln* (Southern Illinois University Press, 2007), he utilized valuable new letters he had discovered. In the present volume, he makes available the text of those documents and the dramatic story of their recovery from historical oblivion. Emerson deserves the thanks of all Lincolnians."

—MICHAEL BURLINGAME, author of *Abraham Lincoln: A Life*

"This companion to [Emerson's *The Madness of Mary Lincoln*] contains both the voice of Mary herself as well as an account of the (largely successful) contemporary efforts to silence her. Those wishing to retrace Emerson's detective work will find this illuminating."

—PATRICK A. LEWIS, *The Register of the Kentucky Historical Society*

"Jason Emerson is a rising star in Lincoln studies, and this volume is further evidence that those of us who never tire of learning about the life and times of Abraham Lincoln are in his debt. This carefully crafted volume illuminates dark corners of Mary Lincoln's life and enhances our understanding of the First Lady after that night at Ford's Theatre."

—MICHAEL S. GREEN, author of *Lincoln and the Election of 1860*

"Emerson portrays Mary realistically but sympathetically [and] dispels the old extreme stereotypes."

—KAREN S. CAMPBELL, editor for the Lincoln Society of Dayton, *Let the Journeys Begin*

"Not only has Jason Emerson uncovered letters by Mary Lincoln, he has uncovered an entire manuscript by James and Myra Bradwell's granddaughter, who tried to use her privileged position to sell the story to the less-discriminating press of her day. It is good to have the Pritchard manuscript in print at last, after eighty hidden years, to have both its insights and its embarrassing sororal prejudices. Emerson, by unearthing a new landmark in the historical treatment of the tragic Mary Lincoln, helps to reconfigure how we view the tragic ex-First Lady"

—**JAMES M. CORNELIUS**, curator of the Abraham Lincoln Presidential Library and Museum

"With this edited volume, Jason Emerson makes an original and valuable contribution to our scholarly understanding of Mary Todd Lincoln's later years. It succeeds and builds on the intriguing and fruitful detective work that the editor achieved in *The Madness of Mary Lincoln*, which provided the most important and original insights into her later years that have been produced in at least the preceding generation. The result is a long-missing yet vital puzzle piece that has long been missing that helps to complete our understanding of Mary Lincoln's commitment proceedings and her eventual release and final difficult years."

—**KENNETH WINKLE**, Thomas C. Sorenson Professor of American History, University of Nebraska-Lincoln

The DARK DAYS *of* ABRAHAM LINCOLN'S WIDOW

As Revealed by Her Own Letters

Dark Days author Myra Helmer Pritchard, granddaughter of James and Myra Bradwell. Courtesy James K. Gordon

The DARK DAYS of ABRAHAM LINCOLN'S WIDOW

As Revealed by Her Own Letters

Myra Helmer Pritchard

Edited and Annotated by Jason Emerson

Southern Illinois University Press / Carbondale

Southern Illinois University Press
www.siupress.com

Printed in the United States of America

26 25 24 23 4 3 2 1

Cover illustration: First Lady Mary Lincoln, as painted in oil by Daniel Huntington, probably in late 1862 or early 1863. Courtesy of the Mary Todd Lincoln House, Lexington, KY.

ISBN 978-0-8093-3924-2 (paperback)
ISBN 978-0-8093-3021-6 (cloth)
ISBN 978-0-8093-8604-8 (ebook)
This book has been catalogued with the Library of Congress.
Library of Congress Control Number: 2023941400

Printed on recycled paper ♻

SIU
Southern Illinois University System

CONTENTS

ACKNOWLEDGMENTS

This book would not have been published without the assistance and permission of Fred C. Towers, Judy Reemtsma, and Dorcy Burns, the children of Frederic N. Towers, Robert T. Lincoln's former attorney, who allowed me complete access to the contents of their father's Lincoln trunk, within which was Pritchard's missing manuscript; James Gordon, the last relative of Myra Pritchard, who allowed me to use and quote from the Myra Pritchard manuscripts in his possession; and the manuscripts division staff at the Library of Congress, where "The Dark Days" manuscript now resides in the manuscripts division.

I'm indebted to the board of trustees of the Mary Todd Lincoln House in Lexington, Kentucky, especially to its director, Gwen Thompson, for allowing me to use a copy of their Mary Lincoln portrait, painted by Daniel Huntington, on the cover of this book. The portrait has never been used in any other publication, as far as any of us could determine.

Special thanks to my mother, Marge Emerson, for inputting Myra Pritchard's 111-page manuscript for me, as it would have taken me innumerable hours to do it myself; to Lincoln scholar Wayne C. Temple for his friendship, advice, and encouragement; to my editor, Sylvia Frank Rodrigue, for indulging me yet again; to the staff of the Cazenovia, New York, public library for all of their assistance; to Chris and Leslie Meyer for accommodating me on my visit to Fredericksburg, Virginia; to Drew and Trisha Long for accommodating me in Washington, D.C.; and to my girls, Kathleen and Olivia, without whose love and encouragement nothing is possible.

EDITOR'S INTRODUCTION

Mary Lincoln is one of the most fascinating—and most written about—First Ladies in American history. She has many admirers, as well as numerous detractors. The former group typically lionizes her as a strong, proud, intelligent woman who was her husband's political partner—even the true intellect and power behind the presidency—resented by the men of her time and misunderstood by the men of today. The latter group sees her as a shrew and a harpy whose sheer unpleasantness drove her husband out of the house and into greatness; they see her as a selfish, petulant, insane egomaniac with few positive qualities. The truth about Mary Lincoln, as is so often the case in history, lies somewhere in the middle.

The vast bibliography concerning Mary Lincoln's life began by portraying her as a mere side character within Abraham Lincoln's heroic American legend. As the years passed and historians began to delve deeper into the makings of Abraham Lincoln's personality, failures, and achievements, his wife's life and influence began to take on greater meaning and to involve further research. She thus began to merit her own examinations, first as the wife of her husband and later as her own person. Typical of history, historians, journalists, and popular culture, it was the controversial aspects of Mary's life that ultimately were pulled to the forefront: her mercurial temper, her extravagant spending, and, more than anything else, her commitment to an insane asylum in 1875. Mary's "insanity" has since become her greatest legacy, and even people who otherwise know nothing about her know that she was "crazy." It was because of this negative and unfairly Manichaean perception about the widow of Lincoln that Myra Helmer Pritchard wrote her book manuscript

"The Dark Days of Abraham Lincoln's Widow, as Revealed by Her Own Letters" in 1927. It would have been a revolutionary—even revelatory—work of American history, had it ever been published.

Myra Helmer Pritchard was the granddaughter of Myra Bradwell, an icon of female and legal activism and one of Mary Lincoln's good friends. In the years after Abraham Lincoln's assassination, Mary spent much time visiting with and writing to the Bradwell family, and Myra's husband James Bradwell acted at times as her attorney. Mary gave them numerous gifts of items connected to her martyred husband, including the pen with which he supposedly signed the Emancipation Proclamation. After Mary was declared insane by a Chicago jury and committed to an asylum by her oldest son, Robert, in 1875, it was Myra and James Bradwell who assisted Mary Lincoln in achieving an early release from Bellevue Place sanitarium despite the protests of her doctor and her son. The story of this event and this friendship—from the Bradwell family point of view—will be explained in the present work. But how this book was written and ultimately suppressed requires its own explanation.

Mary Lincoln wrote more than thirty letters to her friend Myra Bradwell and about a half dozen to James Bradwell, all between 1867 and 1878.[1] The Bradwells kept these in their possession and eventually passed them down through the family. The Bradwells' daughter, Bessie Bradwell Helmer, came into possession of the Lincoln materials after her father's death in 1907. To her, these letters were not only mementos from a family friend but also evidence refuting the poor reputation of a maligned historical figure. Bessie passed these letters, along with her own memories of Mary Lincoln and belief in Mary's sanity, to her daughter Myra Helmer Pritchard and asked that one day they be used to vindicate Mary Todd Lincoln's reputation. "These letters along with some other Lincoln relics were given to me some eight or nine years before my mother's death, with the stipulation that I should write about them but not until both my mother and Robert Lincoln should have passed on," Pritchard later wrote. "My mother was most anxious that these letters be published because she felt that Mrs. Abraham Lincoln had been maligned and that these letters would explain much of the real Mrs. Lincoln to the world and place her in a more favorable light."[2]

Robert Lincoln died in July 1926. After Bessie Helmer died in January 1927, Myra Pritchard immediately set to work. One of her first actions was to show the letters to Chicago judge Henry Horner, one of the great collectors of Lincolniana, to ask his opinion of their historical value. He told her the letters would have "an unquestioned bearing on the phases of history in which [Mary Lincoln] played a part."[3] She previously had showed the letters to family friend and amateur historian Eleanor Gridley, who also pronounced them extremely valuable.[4]

When Pritchard began her book, she knew the subject would be not just a historical but also a publishing boon. By 1927 there never had been a book published solely about Mary Lincoln's life; and of the books that did mention her within the larger story of her husband or the Civil War, only a few briefly mentioned her trial and institutionalization. This paucity of writings about Mary Lincoln is evidenced in the frustration that some of her early biographers suffered during their research. "It is an astounding thing to contemplate," Honoré Willsie Morrow wrote in 1928, "the fact that Lincoln could grow to the god-like proportions he has attained in people's minds and so little be said about his wife."[5] A few years later, Dr. W. A. Evans encountered the same roadblock. "One day I went to a library and asked the attendant to give me what she had dealing with Mrs. Lincoln. When the material was produced, it dealt principally with Mr. Lincoln; there was little about his wife. I turned most of it back, saying, 'I am not looking for material on Mr. Lincoln now. I am making a study of Mrs. Lincoln,'" to which the attendant asked why.[6]

Pritchard secured a contract in April 1927 with J. H. Sears & Company to publish her work in nine installments in *Liberty* magazine, for which she was paid five thousand dollars.[7] These articles were to be later compiled into a book. This journey from magazine to book, typical of the early twentieth century, was one that previously had served journalist Ida Tarbell well: her series of articles on Abraham Lincoln in *McClure's Magazine* in the 1890s doubled the magazine's subscriptions, led to a multivolume book, and began a successful career for Tarbell as a Lincoln historian.[8]

In October 1927, after completing her manuscript, Pritchard and her attorney, N. Otis Rockwood, traveled to Manchester, Vermont, to call on Mary Harlan Lincoln, Robert Lincoln's widow. The visit was a courtesy call—arranged by Rockwood, who was a friend of Lincoln attorney Frederic N. Towers—to inform the family of the pending publication of the Lincoln-Bradwell letters as historical narrative. Towers related the "surprise party" visit a few days later to Katherine Helm, Robert Lincoln's cousin, who was at that time in the midst of writing the family-authorized biography of Mary Lincoln:

> Mrs. Pritchard contemplates the publication of this material, in the form of a biographical sketch; and while, of course, she does not have to ask anyone's permission to do so, the purpose of her visit here was to inform Mrs. Lincoln of her intention; which, I think, is very decent of her. She tacitly agreed to submit to Mrs. Lincoln's inspection anything she might wish to publish; and Mrs. Lincoln, I believe, rather feels as I do,—namely, that it is better to have Mrs. Pritchard as a friend than to offend her. So she has agreed, tentatively, to see Mrs. Pritchard in Washington.[9]

In fact, Mary Harlan Lincoln not only agreed to meet with Mrs. Pritchard in Washington, D.C., but also suggested that she may be able to add information from her own files and perhaps to connect Pritchard with Katherine Helm for a mutually beneficial meeting.[10]

After reading the manuscript, however, Mary Harlan Lincoln decided the story could not and should not be published as it was written. She knew her husband's sense of family propriety and privacy had led him to collect and destroy as many letters of his mother's "period of mental derangement" as he could.[11] To Robert, these letters were not only private family matters; they also were embarrassing to the Lincoln family legacy. Myra Pritchard herself later wrote, "One can readily see why the Robert Lincolns would not want these letters published."[12]

With this understanding, Frederic Towers met with Myra Pritchard in Washington in December 1927 to discuss the situation. During the two-day conference, Towers informed Pritchard that Mary Harlan Lincoln found three of the Mary Todd Lincoln letters in the manuscript "unfair and . . . objectionable" to print.[13] The two parties discussed the possibility of removing the specific letters from the manuscript, but Pritchard ultimately refused, believing it "would somewhat divest the story of its commercial value."[14] Unfortunately for Pritchard, she was in a legal bind because of a recent court decision that the writer of a letter, and his or her succeeding heirs, not the recipient, was the actual owner.[15] Since Mary Harlan Lincoln would not consent to publication without revisions, and Pritchard did not want to get sued, it was suggested that the entire manuscript, the original letters, and any copies should be sold either to the Lincoln family or to "some friendly publishing company, to be revised, printed or destroyed as might be seen fit."[16]

Finding herself with no options, Pritchard agreed to a full sale of the material and all copies for the price of $22,500—a compromise between the $20,000 Mary Harlan Lincoln felt appropriate and the $25,000 Myra Pritchard thought reasonable.[17] The sale was conditional upon authentication of the letters by a handwriting expert, which was secured and confirmed in late January 1928 from the examiner of questioned documents at the U.S. Treasury department.[18]

The actual contract of sale, executed on January 31, 1928, set the conditions that the manuscript and all connected letters, and all copies, in Myra Pritchard's possession be turned over to Mary Lincoln; that no other person had any copies of the materials; that no other copies of the materials existed; that if Myra Pritchard subsequently obtained any other Lincoln family letters they would be turned over to the Lincoln family; that Myra Pritchard would not publish, or permit or cause to be published, any of the manuscript or letters in her possession; and that if any of the materials were published or offered for sale, in whole or part, by anyone who secured possession through Myra Pritchard, the contract would be voided and she would be required to repay the Lincoln family the amount of purchase.[19]

The contract "sews her up as tight as a drum," observed Karl Harriman, the vice president of Myra Pritchard's publishers, J. H. Sears & Company, once he was informed of it. "In point of fact I think if she is apprehended reading a book about Lincoln, or mentioning his name or the name of his lady, she is likely to subject herself thereby to imprisonment for life, if indeed not summary execution."[20] Myra Pritchard and the general manager of Liberty Weekly, Inc., signed a contract dissolving their previous publishing agreement in January 1928.[21]

Pritchard did not know what Mary Harlan Lincoln intended to do with the letters, but she assumed they would be destroyed.[22] Perhaps it was for that reason that she, against the constraints of the contract, kept copies of all the letters as well as her unpublished manuscript. Despite this deceit, which was perhaps more personal than anything else, she firmly upheld the rest of her deal. When Pritchard received letters in late November 1928 seeking access to her family letters, she wrote to Frederic Towers and asked him how to respond.[23] "It is my desire to protect your interests in every way I can," she wrote. Towers suggested she answer honestly and simply say the papers "have passed out of your hands."[24] In 1929 Lincoln collector Henry Horner—who had assisted Myra Pritchard in her book research—asked if she would share her Mary Lincoln knowledge and stories with Carl Sandburg, who was then in the midst of writing his own Lincoln-related book projects and whom Horner had told the saga of the Bradwell-Lincoln letters. "While [Sandburg] realizes that the subject matter of the letters is no longer public property, yet, he is wondering if you would deem it proper to tell him something about the substance of them. Would you do so?" Horner asked. "You may be assured that he would not use this in any manner which might bring forth any criticism of you." Pritchard agreed.[25] Then in 1932, when Pritchard donated other Lincoln items in her possession on a call-loan basis to the Chicago Historical Society for public display, she made sure no statement or record was made of the letters previously in her possession.[26]

The secret was kept until Pritchard's death in February 1947. At that time, her daughter Margreta Pritchard found herself in possession of her mother's safety deposit box and discovered inside a parcel labeled "In case of my death this is to be destroyed immediately." The parcel contained the entire 1928 *Liberty* magazine manuscript. After Margreta Pritchard read the manuscript, she told her family members her intention and "personally burn[ed] the contents and entirely consumed the same in flames."[27] She did not, however, burn the typewritten copies of the letters. Instead, she approached Oliver R. Barrett, one of the foremost Lincoln collectors in America, to ask his advice on whether or not she should publish the letters. There is no evidence to explain why Margreta Pritchard considered publishing the letters against her mother's previous contract with the Lincoln family, and no way to know how the Lincolns would have reacted. Mary Harlan Lincoln had died in 1937, but her children and grandchildren were still alive, as was Frederic Towers, who negotiated the deal and still had the papers in his possession.[28]

Barrett advised Margreta Pritchard that the letters should not be published, that it would not be "exactly morally right" to publish letters that Robert Lincoln so aggressively sought to keep private and unpublished during his life, and to which his family had taken the time and expense to purchase, presumably so they could be destroyed. He said that they had "absolutely no historical value" and would be of benefit only to someone "who desired to read the rantings of an insane person." He also told Pritchard's attorneys to thoroughly search her belongings to obtain the typewritten copies of the letters, the manuscript and any evidence of the fact that the originals were sold to the Lincoln family. "He then feels that we should take these typewritten copies and tie them together securely and place a screw through the middle of them and then get in touch with the Librarian of the Library of Congress and the President of the Chicago Historical Society and in their presence have the same destroyed."[29] Margreta Pritchard's attorneys agreed with Barrett for the same reasons and urged her to destroy the letters, which she ultimately did.[30]

Throughout this twenty-year period between the deaths of Bessie Bradwell Helmer and Myra Helmer Pritchard, the Bradwell-Lincoln letters had become famous in Lincoln lore. Multiple historians had tried and failed to find them, including W. A. Evans, a Mary Lincoln biographer, and William Slade, chief of bibliography at the Library of Congress, in 1928, and Ruth Painter Randall, another Mary biographer, in 1948.[31] It generally was believed the correspondence had been destroyed, but scholars wondered if it didn't still exist somewhere, hidden from history's prying eyes. In fact, it did, and it was. Copies of nearly everything survived and were placed in a steamer trunk of Lincoln family documents owned by family attorney Frederic N. Towers. Whether Towers saved these documents under direction of Mary Harlan Lincoln, or more likely, unknown to Mrs. Lincoln as a way to preserve history, is unclear.

I discovered the Towers trunk in 2005 after a five-month search, the result of my own research on the life of Robert T. Lincoln.[32] After first writing my own book based on the Bradwell-Lincoln correspondence, my publisher and I agreed that Myra Pritchard's unpublished book should finally see the light of day after more than eighty years in the darkness. Legally, no issues or objections could be found to discourage this decision; morally, the question came down to, should a book suppressed by the Lincoln family be published?[33] Since so much has been printed on this topic already—including my previous book, which uses much of the same material in this book—and this work contains new information that further illuminates Mary Lincoln's insanity case and augments the previous studies of the topic, my decision was yes. The job of the historian is to examine and illuminate past events, to explain why events happened and why they matter to us today, and of course the best way to do that is by finding new and previously unpublished materials that enhance our knowledge and understanding.

Pritchard's manuscript is presented here with her original title, some minor editing to modernize her outdated punctuation style, explanatory notations on right-hand pages, and documentary notes at the back of the book.

Pritchard's book, *The Dark Days of Abraham Lincoln's Widow, as Revealed by Her Own Letters*, is a fascinating work. As the title states, it is biography through correspondence. But it is more than that. To a certain degree it is the telling of a long-held family tale of the most extraordinary episode in Mary Lincoln's life, using many Bradwell family anecdotes and beliefs that are published no place else. The book is also, in its own way, a sort of defense brief against the notion of Mary Lincoln's insanity and the propriety of committing her to an insane asylum. Myra Pritchard clearly did not believe Mary Lincoln was insane, nor did Bessie Bradwell Helmer, and it seems as though Myra Bradwell did not either, although she often spoke out of both sides of her mouth on the issue, depending on her immediate goals.

Pritchard's work does have its shortcomings. The main one is simply the lack of historical records on which Pritchard could draw for research, which has been previously mentioned, and her errors and omissions as a result. But for an amateur historian Pritchard did well in her work and clearly read and often quoted from the major Lincoln writers between 1865 and 1927, weaving their facts and interpretations regarding Mary Lincoln into her narrative. I have attempted to fill in all the factual gaps through my notations. The second major detriment to the work is Pritchard's clear bias and apologetic tone in favor of Mary Lincoln. This is not surprising, since Mary was a family friend, but friendship and history do not always make good bedfellows. If Myra Pritchard had spent some time trying to understand exactly why Mary Lincoln was committed in the first place—her range and duration of symptoms, the opinions of the physicians as well as family and friends, and Robert Lincoln's motivations behind his actions—this may have been a much different book. At the very least, how I wish Pritchard had sought out Robert or Mary Harlan Lincoln and asked for their assistance, or even for a collaboration with them or their historian-cousin Katherine Helm—who knows what unknown information might have been revealed! Of course, such a path into the Lincoln family's confidence might also have killed Pritchard's book before it was even begun, just as it killed it after it was finished.

Considering that Pritchard's text is flawed by her bias and her occasional factual inaccuracies, the question also has been raised about the scholarly propriety of publishing such a work. The risk becomes one of disseminating incorrect information about Mary Lincoln (especially if readers do not read the clarifying annotations). I agree this is a risk, but I think the benefits of Pritchard's manuscript outweigh the dangers. *Dark Days* is an important contribution to what we know about Mary Lincoln—the Bradwell family reminiscences of her in the text are unique, as are some of the newspaper articles quoted herein that were preserved by Myra Bradwell herself and missed by subsequent historians. Pritchard's writing also offers a glimpse into the state of historical scholarship on Mary as it was in the 1920s, and how Mary Lincoln generally was viewed by the public. It is clear from the text of this book, as well as the first few published books about Mary in 1928 and 1932, that she had a poor reputation and was more maligned than she was admired. She was, in a word, misunderstood. *Dark Days*, then, furthers our understanding of Mary and of her bibliography. It makes us cognizant of a relatively unknown aspect of her life—her relationship with the Bradwells—and allows us a glimpse into the earliest makings of Mary's historical reputation. Of course, a previously unpublished book containing previously unpublished letters (but subsequently published in my 2007 book, *The Madness of Mary Lincoln*) by, for, and about such an important historical figure is, in one sense, reason enough by itself to support publication.Since *The Dark Days of Abraham Lincoln's Widow* is Myra Pritchard's book and not mine, I have not attempted to rewrite her work, only to edit and annotate to better clarify and explain her interpretations, information, and source materials. I strongly urge the reader to consult these annotations. Of course, I could not insert all the details about Mary Lincoln's institutionalization that I have revealed in my own research—especially concerning Robert Lincoln's motivations behind it—and so I do, in all humility, suggest interested readers also see my book *The Madness of Mary Lincoln*, which also was based on the long-hidden Lincoln-Bradwell correspondence but which does contain a more balanced approach to the story utilizing a broader palette of source material.

The DARK DAYS of ABRAHAM LINCOLN'S WIDOW

As Revealed by Her Own Letters

1

My grandfather, Judge James B. Bradwell of Chicago, was Mrs. Abraham Lincoln's attorney before, during, and after the period she was incarcerated, at the instigation of her son Robert T. Lincoln, in Dr. R[ichard] J. Patterson's private hospital for the insane [Bellevue Place] at Batavia, Illinois. During this time—from 1872 to 1878—Mrs. Lincoln carried on an extensive correspondence with my grandfather and Myra Bradwell, his wife, the latter an intimate and deeply sympathetic friend of President Lincoln's widow.

These letters have been in my possession several years, but, because of reasons I shall explain, I could not make them public sooner. They are decidedly historic—even startlingly so—else I should not publish them at all, for, to me, they are sacred. In them I see the poignant record of a woman's sorrow and disillusionment, a record to be protected from prying eyes were it not for the fact that even the heartaches of the great are public property.

Abraham Lincoln, his life and his work, his wife and his children, all are of paramount interest to Americans. Thousands of volumes concerning the martyred President have been published, but the Lincoln literature has been comparatively silent regarding the little woman who bore his name.[a] When it has not been silent it usually has been harshly critical of her character and disposition. Scant sympathy has been accorded her, and there seems to be a strange lack of realization that the many tragedies and great sorrows which came to her during life might be indirectly accountable for her outbursts of temperament.

This seems to be the era of the past in the interest of the reading public. Lincolniana, particularly, has been diligently studied; searched with a

1

a. When Myra Pritchard wrote her book in 1926–27, there were no biographies of Mary Lincoln then published. Mary had been mentioned in a few memoirs by people acquainted with her, such as Mary Clemmer Ames, Rebecca Pomroy, Adam Badeau, and William O. Stoddard. She also had been mentioned in various biographies of her husband, most notably the largely negative portrayals in the biographies by Ward H. Lamon (1872) and William Herndon (1889). The two most in-depth examinations of Mary Lincoln prior to Pritchard's book were the 1868 book by Mary's White House seamstress, Elizabeth Keckley, *Behind the Scenes: Thirty Years a Slave and Four Years in the White House*, and William E. Barton's 1927 book *The Women Lincoln Loved*. Two other well-done analyses of Mary in this period were Ida M. Tarbell's two-volume *Life of Abraham Lincoln* (1900) and Gamaliel Bradford's book on the spouses of famous men, *Wives* (1925).

literary microscope. I think it is safe to say that, today, there are few, if any, manuscripts, documents, or letters pertaining to President Lincoln and his family which have not been given to the world and published in their entirety.[b]

To my knowledge there are two exceptions: the package of letters and documents belonging to President Lincoln and deposited with the government by his son, Robert T. Lincoln, with the stipulation that they should not be opened until twenty-five years after the latter's death; and the letters to be published in this series—Mary Todd Lincoln's letters to my grandparents.[c]

The reason for Robert T. Lincoln's request is not known. There are many rumors![d]

Mrs. Lincoln's letters have not been published owing to the request of my mother, Bessie Bradwell Helmer, that they should not be given to the public until after the death of Robert T. Lincoln and herself.[3] After one has perused the letters, the reason for her request is, I think, obvious.

Prior to the time of Mrs. Lincoln's detention at Batavia, her mental status had occasioned considerable controversy. Lawyers and physicians presented legal and medical evidence to a jury of prominent Chicago citizens to the effect that Mrs. Lincoln was insane. She was declared to be a lunatic and ordered detained as such.[e]

During this most critical period of her life few people of influence befriended her or gave themselves the trouble of investigating her side of the question. For this reason my mother stipulated that after her death and that of Robert T. Lincoln the documents to be set forth here, which were given her by her father, Judge Bradwell, were to be published. She wanted the present generation, so interested in Lincolnian literature, to be familiar with the protestations of a practically friendless woman.[f]

Within the past year Robert T. Lincoln and my mother died, and I am complying with her request by writing this series of articles.[g]

My grandmother, Myra Bradwell, to whom many of the letters were written, was the first woman in the modern world to apply for admission to the bar.[h] In 1868 she founded the *Chicago Legal News* and was its editor until 1894, when she died. My grandfather, who came to Chicago in

b. Pritchard of course had no way to know at the time how utterly incorrect she was. To this day, historians continue to find unknown and unpublished Lincoln manuscripts in various locations, while private individuals also continue to come forward and donate family items. These discoveries and donations increased dramatically after the opening of the Abraham Lincoln Presidential Library and Museum in Springfield, Illinois, in April 2005 and because of the national Lincoln Bicentennial Celebration from 2008 through 2010.

c. Robert Lincoln deposited his father's personal and presidential papers in the Library of Congress on May 8, 1919, for safekeeping, although he retained ownership and sole control over access. He formally donated the papers, now known as The Robert Todd Lincoln Collection of the Papers of Abraham Lincoln, to the United States of America, "to be deposited in the Library of Congress for the benefit of all the People," on January 23, 1923. A condition of his deed was that the papers would be sealed from public view until twenty-one years (not twenty-five) after his death.[1]

d. Robert stated many times this was because individuals mentioned in the papers, or their descendents, still were living, and it would be improper to expose them or their private views to public scrutiny. This was a typical attitude for a Victorian-era gentleman such as Robert who believed strongly in the tenet of personal privacy. Historian David C. Mearns wrote that some people believed the condition was a way for Robert to thwart historian Albert J. Beveridge from obtaining access to the papers, about which Beveridge pestered Robert for years. Robert's refusal to grant Beveridge access to the papers stated his privacy concerns and impugned nothing personal.[2]

e. Mary Lincoln was declared insane by a Chicago jury on May 19, 1875. The trial received national newspaper attention, but the local Chicago papers naturally had the best coverage.[4]

f. "My mother was most anxious that these letters be published because she felt that Mrs. Abraham Lincoln had been maligned and that these letters would explain much of the real Mrs. Lincoln to the world and place her in a more favorable light," Pritchard wrote.[5]

g. Robert Lincoln died July 26, 1926; Bessie Bradwell Helmer died Jan. 10, 1927. Pritchard contracted with *Liberty Weekly* magazine on April 6, 1927 to write a series of serialized articles about Mary Lincoln based on the letters in her possession. This series afterward was to be arranged into a book.[6]

h. She was actually the second woman. Six weeks before Bradwell applied in August 1869, teacher Arabella Mansfield applied and was admitted to the Iowa bar. Mansfield had no interest in the law, however, and no intention of ever practicing law. Her application for admission was simply part of a plan

1834, then became the editor and publisher of the News and was active in its direction until a short time before his death in 1907.

Bessie Bradwell Helmer, my mother, a lawyer and the only woman ever to edit the revised statutes of Illinois, took over the publication and, with my father, attorney Frank A. Helmer, conducted it in accordance with the policies established by its founder.[8]

The offices of the News contained many mementoes of the Lincolns, keepsakes I remember very vividly. Even as a child I knew these were precious tokens from the past and I stood a little in awe of them. Years later I was allowed to read Mary Todd Lincoln's letters and to hold the relics of her illustrious husband she had given my grandparents.

There is the gold mounted pen with which he signed the immortal Proclamation of Emancipation. I am aware of several other claims to ownership of this historic pen but, since the one now in my possession was authenticated by Mary Lincoln herself, I am convinced of its genuineness.[9]

Mrs. Lincoln also gave my grandmother the green stone [known generally as the "bloodstone seal"] presented to the President by the Sultan of Turkey; but the most precious of all is Abraham Lincoln's definition of democracy.[i] It is in his own handwriting, signed with his characteristic "A. Lincoln," and reads:

"As I would not be a slave, so I would not be a master—This expresses my idea of democracy—Whatever differs from this, to the extent of the difference, is no democracy—"[j]

I have underlined and inserted dashes here just as they appear in the original.

As items of Lincolniana these, I suppose, are priceless, but, for me, the dearest of them all are Mary Todd Lincoln's letters. After all, Lincoln's fame, his place in the hearts of his fellow men, is secure, above reproach, but Mary Todd Lincoln has scarcely been heard at all, as yet. When her sorrow was the deepest, people hurt her most; when her hopes were at lowest ebb, they gave her the least sympathy.

The truth is not always agreeable, but in matters such as this, it is history. Mr. Herndon in vindicating the writing of such a frank life of Lincoln speaks of the time when the president had just finished reading

devised by Iowa judge Francis Springer as a way to promote the equality of women. So Bradwell is considered the "first" because she actually intended to become a practicing attorney. After Bradwell passed the Illinois bar exam with high honors in 1869, she was denied a license to practice by the state bar. Both the Illinois Supreme Court and the U.S. Supreme Court upheld the denial.[7]

i. Myra Pritchard loaned these and other Lincoln-related items to the Chicago Historical Society for temporary yet indefinite public display in 1932. Her daughter, Margreta Pritchard, sold them to Lincoln collector Oliver R. Barrett in 1947. The Definition of Democracy and the Emancipation pen now are part of the Lincoln Collection in the Abraham Lincoln Presidential Library and Museum in Springfield, Illinois.[10]

j. Roy P. Basler, in his edition of Abraham Lincoln's collected works, verified that the Bradwells owned the "Definition," and that it was a gift from Mary Lincoln. In 1895 James B. Bradwell gave an interview with the *Chicago Times-Herald* specifically about Lincoln's definition of democracy, his interpretation and opinion of it, and the associations with Lincoln's life and death it brought to mind. "I have here, from his own hand, his definition of democracy—and it seems to me still the best definition that could be made," Bradwell said. "The absolute sense of equality which underlies this sentiment seems to have been a keynote of the man's character. It was not so much that Lincoln believed in the unalterable equality of all men—for the truth that all men are created equal does not involve that doctrine—but that he believed unalterably in an equity which insured to each man, of whatever race, precisely that reward which his labors could earn for him."[11] Interestingly, nowhere in this interview—including his reminiscences of Lincoln's death and Chicago funeral—did Bradwell state or imply any personal relationship with the president.

the life of Edmund Burke. He closed the volume, tossed it upon the table, and exclaimed,

"It's like all the others. Biographies as generally written are not only misleading but false. The author of this life of Burke makes a wonderful hero of his subject. He magnifies his perfections—if he had any—and suppresses his imperfections. He is so faithful in his zeal and so lavish in praise of his every act that one is almost driven to believe that Burke never made a mistake or a failure in his life.

"Billy, I've wondered why book publishers and merchants don't have blank biographies on their shelves, always ready for an emergency; so that, if a man happens to die, his heirs and his friends, if they wish to perpetuate his memory, can purchase one already written, but with blanks. These blanks they can at their pleasure fill up with rosy sentences full of high-sounding praise. In most instances they commemorate a lie and cheat posterity out of the truth."

Mr. Herndon then adds, "This emphatic avowal of sentiment from Mr. Lincoln not only fixes his estimate of ordinary biography but is my vindication in advance, if assailed, for writing the truth."[12] [k]

May I express the same sentiments as those of Mr. Herndon in publishing these letters?

As a starting point we should, I think, recall some of the more intimate details of Mary Todd Lincoln's early life. Hers was a long line of distinguished ancestors. Her paternal grandfather succeeded Daniel Boone in command of the militia, and her maternal great grandfather, Andrew Porter, was a general in the Revolutionary War. Her great uncles, George and David Porter, were governors of Michigan and Pennsylvania, respectively, and her father, Robert S. Todd, had served in both houses of the Kentucky legislature and for twenty years was president of the bank at Lexington. So much for family trees.[l]

Mary Todd was a creature of moods and was swayed by a fierce, quick temper. Were she a modern girl she would be looked upon as the victim of endocrine disturbances, functional psychosis, hidden complexes, or, perhaps, the possessor—not the victim—of that greatly prized quality known as temperament.[m] Yet beneath it all was a deep affection for those she really loved, and her heart was torn and scarred by the series of

k. Herndon's definition of "truth" in his historical work is its own controversy. He believed in the "warts and all" approach to history in which airing a man's faults and foibles was to show the full and true man. This was at a time when nearly everything written about Lincoln was sanitized hagiography, and Herndon's "honesty" was therefore highly condemned. Arguably no one has done more to illuminate the life of Lincoln than William Herndon, and yet his writings are vitiated by the sanctimony of his own superiority as a historian. Understanding Herndon, his opinions, methods, and motives is in fact its own subset of Lincoln studies; while Herndon's relationship with and writing and opinions about Mary Lincoln is a further category. There have been no more enduringly damning words about Mary written than those of Herndon's; and yet he honestly believed that in his criticism of her and his statements that Lincoln never loved her, he was actually doing Mary a *favor*, because he felt the truth would be told one day anyway, so to have it come from a family friend would be easier.[13]

l. For a good history of the Todd clan, see Stephen Berry, *House of Abraham: Lincoln & the Todds, a Family Divided by War* (Boston: Houghton Mifflin, 2007), and William H. Townsend, *Lincoln and His Wife's Home Town* (Indianapolis: Bobbs-Merrill, 1929).

m. Contemporary medical and historical opinion leans toward the theory that Mary suffered bipolar disorder, although previous theories have included migraine, general "personality disorder," posttraumatic stress, and even syphilis.[14]

tragic events that befell her beloved husband, her children, and herself in later years.[n]

The world in general may not have seen it, but hers was a nature peculiarly sensitive to the finer values of life. She might lose herself in a fit of ungovernable temper, but there was no one who could be more deeply touched by the sorrows of a friend.

Impetuously, when she was but twenty-one, she left her home in Kentucky when she found a stepmother irksome and irritating. She fled to the home of her sister Mrs. Ninian Edwards in Springfield, Illinois, and, almost immediately, her position as a reigning belle in society there was assured.[o]

She had many suitors, and among the most ardent were Stephen A. Douglas and Abraham Lincoln, then a struggling young lawyer. She accepted the latter, much to the dissatisfaction of her family. Oh, little Mary Todd, to become famous and almost infamous from the acrimonious criticism of so many misunderstanding folk; what a breadth of vision was yours to perceive the dynamic possibilities in the lanky young giant who pleaded his suit so awkwardly nearly a century ago!

Had you accepted Stephen Douglas or some other handsome gallant who could have given you immediate fortune and social security, the name and glorious companionship of one of the nation's mightiest patriots would not have been yours; but is it not possible you would have been spared the heartaches and overwhelming tragedies of later years? The road of life surely would have been less difficult, albeit less interesting.

But she did accept Lincoln, who brought her the greatest humiliation she yet had had to bear by jilting her. She was bitterly humiliated—heartbroken—for rumor had it that the thoroughly conscientious Lincoln had remained away from his own wedding because he was not certain of the compatibility of their union. Herndon maintains this, but other authorities offer rather convincing evidence that this was not so.[p]

They quote the emphatic denials of such persons as Mrs. B. S. Edwards, sister-in-law of Ninian Edwards, where Mary made her home, and "Cousin Lizzie Grimsley Brown," wife of Dr. Brown of Springfield. Miss [Ida M.] Tarbell also quotes Mrs. John [Todd] Stuart, wife of Major Stuart, at one time associated with Lincoln in the law, and Mrs. [Frances Todd] Wallace, sister of Mary Todd, as vehemently denying this rumor.[17]

n. Mary Lincoln's was a life full of tragedy. When Mary was six her mother died; in a span of six months between 1849 and 1850, Mary's father, maternal grandmother, and four-year-old son Edward Baker Lincoln all died; eleven-year-old son Willie died in the White House in 1862; Abraham Lincoln was assassinated while Mary sat beside him holding his hand in 1865; and her youngest boy Thomas "Tad" Lincoln died in 1871 at age seventeen.

o. Mary was actually age twenty when she moved into the Edwards home in October 1839. She was beautiful, charming, witty, cultured, and intelligent—and the bachelors of the town certainly noticed. "Mary was quick, gay and in the social world somewhat brilliant," said her sister, Elizabeth Edwards. Lawyer James Conkling said, "She is the very creature of excitement," while Mary's brother-in-law Ninian Edwards famously said of her, "She could make a bishop forget his prayers."[15]

p. Herndon created and perpetuated this story, but the historical evidence and other eyewitness accounts prove this to be a fiction. Lincoln did not leave Mary standing at the altar on their wedding day. He did break off their engagement due to his own insecurities about being a good husband and good family provider, especially to a woman of such a wealthy and aristocratic background as Mary Todd.[16]

Dr. William Barton, held an authority on all things pertaining to Lincoln, believes that

"The date had not been set for the wedding; that preparations had not gone as far as Herndon describes; that the breaking of the engagement happened as the result of a quarrel . . . and that the rupture was known only to the intimate friends of Lincoln and Mary Todd."[18]

In any case on November 4, 1842, Mary Todd and Abraham Lincoln were married by Rev. Charles N. Dresser. Julia N. Jayne "stood up" with Mary, and James M. Matheny attended the future president.[q] Mr. Matheny, in a letter to Herndon dated August 21, 1888, entertainingly describes the wedding.

"Marriages in Springfield, up to that time, had been rather commonplace affairs. Lincoln's was perhaps the first one ever performed with all the requirements of the Episcopal ceremony.

"A goodly number of friends had gathered and while witnessing the ceremony one of the most amusing incidents imaginable occurred. No description on paper can do it justice. Among those present was Thomas C. Brown, one of the judges of the Supreme Court. He was, in truth, an 'old timer' and had the virtue of saying just what he thought, without regard to place or surroundings. He had been on the bench for many years and was not less rough than quaint and curious.

"There was, of course, the perfect hush in the room as the ceremony progressed. Brown was standing just behind Lincoln. Old Parson Dresser, in canonical robes, with much and impressive solemnity recited the Episcopal service. He handed Lincoln the ring, who, placing it on the bride's finger, repeated the church formula, 'With this ring I thee endow with all my goods and chattels, lands and tenements.'

"Brown, who had never witnessed such a proceeding was struck with its utter absurdity. 'God Almighty, Lincoln!' he ejaculated, loud enough to be heard by all, 'the statute fixed all that!' This unlooked-for interruption almost upset the old parson, who had a keen sense of the ridiculous, and, for the moment, it seemed as if he would break down, but, presently recovering his gravity, he hastily pronounced them husband and wife."[20 r]

Thus were Mary Todd and Abraham Lincoln married.

q. Julia Jayne was a close friend of Mary's in Springfield. Mary and Julia had once coauthored a pseudonymous letter signed "Rebecca," which was published in the Springfield newspaper in 1842 that nearly caused Abraham Lincoln to fight a duel. While Lincoln himself had previously published an anonymous letter attacking the politics of Illinois state auditor James Shields, Mary and Julia offered barbed personal insults in their letter. When Shields demanded the identity of the writer from the newspaper publisher, Lincoln said he had done it. Julia married Lyman Trumbull, a member of the Springfield "coterie" and, like his friend Lincoln, an ambitious politician. In 1855, after Trumbull beat Lincoln for the U.S. Senate seat from Illinois, an offended Mary never spoke to her friend Julia again.[19]

r. Pritchard's transcription here is not a verbatim replication of Matheny's letter as it is in the Herndon-Weik Collection of Lincolniana at the Library of Congress.[21]

The years which followed were not easy ones for the once carefree, brilliant, impetuous belle of Springfield. Children came, four sons in all: Robert Todd on August 1, 1843, and on March 10, three years later, Edward, who lived but a few years, was born. In December 1850 came William Wallace and three years later Thomas, affectionately known as "Tad."

Lincoln's income was limited and, for the first time in her life, Mary Todd knew what it meant to want things and be unable to have them. Even pennies counted in that household. Her turbulent disposition often distressed her husband and sons, but it is only fair to point out that she was often alone, for it was said of Lincoln that "he would stop anywhere with anyone to talk politics."[5]

On November 6, 1860, Abraham Lincoln was elected president of the United States. How that must have thrilled Mary Todd Lincoln! When she took his name people said she had married beneath her station! They smiled and shook their heads and whispered, "I told you so's," when two and three and four babies came. They taunted her covertly, slyly, cruelly with the rich and handsome Douglas. But now—now that same Stephen Douglas was one of her husband's defeated rivals for the presidency just as he had been for her hand!

The sad-eyed man she loved had won, at last. Prosperity and glory were theirs, and one can imagine how the smile returned to her lips, the flash to her eyes as she forgot the tribulations of the past and dreamed of a future dazzlingly bright!

She entertained with a lavish hand, spent large sums on an elaborate wardrobe, but the portals of Washington society did not swing open to her. She was harshly criticized for her "wanton extravagance," for her impetuosity, for the way she managed her children.

Not satisfied with this, her detractors sought to make of her friendly relations with Senator Sumner a flagrant, sordid affair. Mary Lincoln met Charles Sumner, senator from Massachusetts at the Inaugural Ball, and because he was the type of considerate gentleman she had known in Kentucky, she was attracted to him.

Sumner called frequently at the White House, for they had much in common, including a knowledge of French, in which language most of

s. Abraham Lincoln was in fact so frequently absent from home that historian Jean Baker has characterized Mary Lincoln as "a single parent."[22]

A Civil War–era carte de visite of Mary Lincoln as First Lady.
Author's collection

their conversation was conducted. They discussed art, books, the affairs of the world, and to Mary Lincoln, it was a welcome return to the niceties of speech she had been denied so many years. That was all. He was a congenial companion, a friend; but their mere presence together was enough for the gossips of Washington. They wrote anonymous letters to the president, to Mary Lincoln, to Sumner in vain attempts to deprive her of the one real friend she had at the capital.[t]

As the Civil War progressed Mary Lincoln's heartaches increased. Because she was of southern birth her enemies speedily turned this fact into a taunt. They accused her of working against her husband. They said she was a traitor, a spy furnishing information to her brothers in the Confederate Army.[u]

There could be no greater proof of the absurdity of this charge than the statement of Elizabeth Keckley in her book Behind the Scenes. Elizabeth Keckley, a former slave, was Mrs. Lincoln's dressmaker. She was devoted to the president and his wife and revealed many intimate details of their home life. In discussing Mary Lincoln's wartime sympathies she wrote,

"One morning on my way to the White House, I heard that Captain Alexander Todd, one of her brothers, had been killed. I did not like to inform Mrs. Lincoln of his death, judging that it would be painful news to her. I had been in her room but a few minutes when she said, with apparent unconcern, 'Lizzie, I have just heard that one of my brothers has been killed in the war.'

'I also heard the same, Mrs. Lincoln, but hesitated to speak of it, for fear the subject would be a painful one to you.'

'You need not hesitate. Of course, it is but natural that I should feel for one so nearly related to me, but not to the extent that you suppose. He made his choice long ago. He decided against my husband, and through him against me. He has been fighting against us; and since he chose to be our deadly enemy, I see no special reason why I should bitterly mourn his death.'

"I felt relieved, and in subsequent conversations learned that Mrs. Lincoln had no sympathy for the South.

"'Why should I sympathize with the rebels?' she would say. 'Are they not against me? They would hang my husband tomorrow if it was in their

t. Mary wrote numerous letters to Sumner during and after the White House years that attest to their friendship. In one such, she said he was "one of my best friends. For the past four years, he was a constant visitor at the W.H. both in office and drawing room—he appreciated my noble husband and I *learned* to converse with him, with more freedom and confidence than with any of my other friends." Upon hearing of Sumner's death in early 1874, Mary lamented, "I have lost my dearest and best friend."[23]

u. Accusations that Mary was a southern sympathizer or even an active spy wounded her deeply at first, but eventually she claimed to be inured to the gossip and slander against her. Yet when these accusations followed her out of the White House, while she was an aggrieved widow seeking a government pension, the stories infuriated her. After reading one such report in the *Chicago Tribune* about three of her brothers being in the Confederate army, Mary exploded in bitter vituperation that "as she left Kentucky at an early age her sympathies were entirely Republican—that her feelings were entirely with the North during the war, and always. I never failed to urge my husband to be an *extreme* Republican, and now, in the day of my trouble, you see how *this* very party is trying to work against me."[24] Even U.S. senator and former Illinois governor Richard Yates accused Mary of treachery when he declared during an open Senate debate, "Amid all the perils of life, amidst its devastation, amid good and evil report, a woman should be true to her husband."[25]

power, and perhaps gibbet me with him. How, then, can I sympathize with a people at war with me and mine?' She always objected to being thought Southern in feeling."[26]

No Northern mother worked more diligently, more sympathetically for the Union cause than did Mary Lincoln. Hers was the dynamic spirit that brought order out of chaos in the congested, slovenly operated hospitals of Washington. She effaced herself in caring for the blue clad soldiers of the North who had been cruelly hurt by bullets fired, perhaps, by her own neighbors, her own kinsmen. Gone, now, was the arrogance, the hatred of detail. In those dark days Mary Todd Lincoln, the "wantonly extravagant," permitted love and sympathy to lead her into drudgery.[v]

During this period the grim specter of Death she had fought in the Washington hospitals turned to strike at her through one she worshipped. Willie, her son, contracted a severe cold which developed into a complicated fever causing his death. For a month Mary Todd Lincoln denied herself to everyone but her harassed, war-weary husband.[w] Day upon day she paced the echoing, empty rooms of the White House, counting costs, wondering, thinking. Then she turned to Lincoln with a new, fierce affection which, in its very intensity, wore her down, consumed her.[x]

Peace dawned, but it was a red, sullen dawning, for the fires of resentment and revolt still smoldered beneath its horizon. Mary Lincoln was aware of none of the evil things accompanying it. To her it was relief from conditions and events that had stifled, crushed her. They could be happy now, she and the sorrowful man she loved. Heartaches, taunts, veiled insults, all these were of the night that had passed. The day had come and with it, happiness.

There would be balls, parties, the theater. Her dreams began to find fulfillment for, on Friday evening, April 14, 1865, President and Mrs. Lincoln with some friends attended a performance of Our American Cousin.[y] The whole world knows what happened there. John Wilkes Booth shot Abraham Lincoln, the president of the United States, the Great Emancipator who had welded a sundered nation, the man Mary Todd Lincoln loved!

The theater that was to bring her diversion, relaxation, brought her life's greatest tragedy. In it she lost her greatest idol and protector, and life

v. One of the great overlooked aspects of Mary as First Lady was her frequent visits to the military hospitals to visit the wounded soldiers. She brought the men fruit, flowers from the White House conservatory, and other gifts; she wrote letters for the soldiers to their mothers or wives; or she would just sit and visit. Mary did not publicize these visits, which White House secretary William O. Stoddard saw as a lost opportunity for the highly criticized First Lady to improve her reputation. "If she were worldly wise she would carry newspaper correspondents, from two to five, of both sexes, every time she went, and she would have them take shorthand notes of what she says to the sick soldiers and of what the sick soldiers say to her," Stoddard wrote in his war-time diary. "Then she would bring the writers back to the White House, and give them some cake—and coffee, as a rule, and show them the conservatory. By keeping up such a process until every correspondent . . . has been dealt with, say twice, she could somewhat sweeten the contents of many journals and of the secretary's waste basket. The directly opposite course, as she pursues it, has not by any means worked well."[27]

w. Both Willie and Tad became sick in February 1862 from what is now generally agreed to have been typhoid fever, due to contaminated drinking water. Willie was sick for nearly three weeks, and died on February 20. Mary was inconsolable. Her grief was so overwhelming it prompted the president one day to point to the lunatic asylum visible from a White House window and say to his wife, "Mother, do you see that large white building on the hill yonder? Try and control your grief, or it will drive you mad, and we may have to send you there."[28]

x. Emilie (also spelled Emily) Todd Helm, Mary's half-sister, noticed in 1863 that Mary was nervous, excitable, and wrought-up, and that she seemed in constant fear of more sorrows being added to her life. "I believe if anything should happen to you or Robert or Tad it would kill her," Emilie told the president.[29]

y. The Lincolns were accompanied by Maj. Henry Rathbone and Miss Clara Harris. The young couple was invited after multiple others had previously declined, including Gen. and Mrs. Grant.

was never to be the same. She was to live in the past henceforth, for the future could hold no happiness now. Sunny days would never seem again so bright, and joy could only be relative. Those of us who have lost dear ones can sympathize with the stunned and lonely little woman whose husband had always stood between her and the world.

The years which followed were drab indeed. Her funds were low, and she went to New York to raise money by selling some of the finery of which she was so proud in the days of her husband's living greatness. Newspapers attacked her.[z] Congress, when appealed to by Sumner for a pension befitting the widow of Abraham Lincoln, scoffed and made her very sustenance a subject for insulting debate.[aa] She returned to Springfield and spent her time between that city and Chicago, establishing her Chicago home at 375 West Washington Boulevard near her friends—my grandfather and grandmother.[bb]

Robert was a successful lawyer with a wife and family, and Tad, always a comfort to his grieving mother, lived at home with her.[cc] In the summer of 1871 he was stricken with typhoid and died.[dd] Mary Lincoln was entirely crushed by this last tragedy added to a life already full. Then it was that she spent evening after evening at the home of my grandparents, being tenderly comforted by my sympathetic grandmother whom even I remember as a tower of strength in herself.

What intimacies of conversation, what anecdotes of Abraham Lincoln, what glowing reminiscences of the past must have been recounted as the two women sat before the blazing logs! My mother, at that time a tall, spindly girl of thirteen, precocious and interested always in things worthwhile would sit by the hour listening to Mrs. Lincoln narrate tales of the Great Emancipator and the days at the White House.

But hers were gray days now. She was sad always, weighted with a great loneliness and a craving for sympathetic companionship. One thinks of her as desperately anxious not to lose touch with the friends who loved her because she had lost so much that could not be replaced.

This note sounds dolefully in all her letters, and it is particularly poignant in the earliest I have, dated November 1, 1872. It reads,

z. Pritchard refers to the Old Clothes Scandal of 1867 during which Mary Lincoln, believing herself on the brink of poverty, tried to sell some of her old White House gowns and jewelry in New York City. It caused a national sensation in the press, intense ridicule and criticism of Mary Lincoln, and much embarrassment to her family and friends. Some people saw Mary's conduct as evidence of insanity. One newspaper reported that Mary's relatives in Springfield believed this was so. Lincoln estate executor David Davis simply called the sale "an act of insanity," brought on by the "insane delusion" she suffered from poverty. Oldest son Robert was mortified by his mother's actions, and he, too, believed she was "not mentally responsible."[30]

aa. During the Congressional debates, all of the politicians Mary had insulted and otherwise wronged during her tenure as First Lady—which were many—now had power over her. Some opposed her request simply because it was unprecedented: no civilian, let alone the widow of a fallen president, had ever received a pension. Others thought Mary was already wealthy from the receipts of her husband's one-hundred-thousand-dollar estate. Others criticized her unethical conduct in the White House and even accused her of being a Rebel spy. It took five years for Congress to grant her a three-thousand-dollar yearly pension, which was signed by President Grant on July 14, 1870.[31]

bb. Mary never lived in Springfield after the assassination, and she rarely visited. She purchased the house at 375 West Washington Street in Chicago using the remainder of President Lincoln's 1865 salary—about twenty-two thousand dollars—which Congress granted her in March 1866. She was forced to move out and rent the house in 1867 because she could not afford it.

cc. Robert Lincoln married Mary Harlan, daughter of James Harlan, U.S. senator from Iowa and President Lincoln's last secretary of the interior, in 1868. Their first child, a daughter, was named Mary after her paternal grandmother.

dd. Tad became seriously ill in late May or early June 1871, shortly after he and his mother returned to Chicago after nearly three years in Europe. Whether his illness was the result of the trip across the Atlantic or a worsening of a previous condition is unknown. In July he died of pleurisy, an inflammation of the membrane that surrounds the lungs and lines the rib cage. The condition causes shortness of breath but likewise can make breathing extremely painful, and it reduces the ability of the sufferer to move freely. Dr. Milton H. Shutes specifically explained Tad's death this way: "With serious effusion compressing the lungs and crowding the nearby heart, there was not enough oxygen to maintain the life centers of the brain." Dr. W. A. Evans reasoned in 1932 that Tad's fatal pleurisy could have been tubercular in origin.[32]

My dear Mrs. Bradwell:

Please inform me what has become of your own dear self. I am very anxious to see you, and I wish you would call in an evening or two. I can scarcely understand your neglect, dear, kind friend. Come *very soon*; and present my kindest regards to your good husband and your daughter. Before three days have passed I want to have one of our old fashioned chats together. With ever so much love, believe me, always, truly yours,

Mary Lincoln[33]

Isn't there a pathetic note in that, "I can scarcely understand your neglect, dear kind friend," when one considers that it is the widow of Abraham Lincoln speaking? Mary Todd Lincoln, once the sought after, vivacious Kentucky belle writing pitifully, pleadingly of neglect!

Thomas “Tad” Lincoln. Mary Lincoln called her youngest son her “troublesome little sunshine,” while the president called his son the “tyrant of the White House.”[34] During the war Tad’s vitality and hijinks gave humor and comfort to his parents, especially after the death of his brother Willie in 1862. After the assassination, Tad became his mother’s constant companion, as well as her solace. As he grew older and she made plans for him to enter boarding schools, the idea of separation from Tad was terrifying and afflictive to Mary. After the public censure she suffered during the Old Clothes Scandal in October 1867, she miserably told her confidant Elizabeth Keckley, “only my darling Taddie prevents my taking my life.” When Tad died in 1871, Mary was devastated. “My beloved boy, was the idol of my heart and had become my inseparable companion,” she wrote. “My heart is entirely broken for without his presence, the world is complete darkness.” The *Chicago Tribune* called Tad’s death “a fearful blow” to Mary Lincoln, and reported, “her physician dreads that it may produce insanity.”[35]
Photo courtesy Library of Congress, Prints and Photographs Division, call number: PR 13 CN 1972:018.

2

Mary Lincoln has written that visits to Springfield hurt and depressed her because they recalled so vividly the happy, companion-filled days when the youngbloods of Illinois were casting their hearts and their fortunes at her feet. She had turned from them to Lincoln, and during these later visits, he and her boys peopled her thoughts to the exclusion of all others so that she came away wan and heartsick to live for days with dead loved ones and old dreams.[a]

Few people on earth, I think, have been as utterly alone as Mary Lincoln was then. Abraham Lincoln was a solitary man, but his widow was lonelier than he. Lincoln was sufficient unto himself, his solitude was as necessary to his character as his grasp of issues; but aloneness, neglect, these were unnatural, fearsome conditions to her.

The buffetings to which she had been subjected frightened, cowed her. She was supersensitive to real or imagined slights and, realizing this, remained much alone. She retained her love of finery and continued to dress richly. Considered in the light of the times—the middle '70's—she was a wealthy woman and, feeling that a certain dignity and position attached to her as the widow of one of the nation's greatest presidents, she spent lavishly on clothes.[b]

She turned to study, apparently finding a kind of tranquility in her books and a few close friends. Then she became ill and was forced to do without both her books and her friends.[c] This illness is the principal topic of her second letter to my grandmother, Myra Bradwell, under date of Monday, January 26, 1873.

2

a. After her visit to Springfield in December 1865 for her husband's reburial from the public holding vault to a temporary tomb, Mary Lincoln wrote to her friend Mary Jane Welles that the visit "convinced me, that the further removed, I am, the better, it will be, for my *reason*, from that *spot*." Mary in fact owned the Lincolns' old home at the corner of Eighth and Jackson Streets in Springfield but refused to live there.[1]

b. Mary's spending mania was so uncontrolled, her son Robert wrote in 1867, "The simple truth, which I cannot tell anyone not personally interested, is that my mother is on one subject not mentally responsible." Mary's sister, Elizabeth Edwards, told Robert that Mary had a habit of reckless spending, stating, "[I]t has always been a prominent trait in her character, to accumulate a large amount of clothing." Artist Francis B. Carpenter, who stayed in the White House for six months while he painted a portrait of the first reading of the Emancipation Proclamation, said Mary "was extravagantly fond of dress, and had more gowns than opportunities to wear them." Mary also reveled in giving gifts to Robert and his family, especially for baby Mamie. The Robert Lincolns accepted the widow's gifts sometimes willingly and sometimes grudgingly. Robert once even wrote they were "frightened" by the ostentation of some baby clothes Mary had sent, to which his mother resentfully replied that it was "not too much, for people in *our station* of life."[2]

c. Mary Lincoln suffered myriad physical ailments her entire life, although some of her complaints seem likely to have been a result of hypochondria as well. As she grew older, her physical complaints included weak nerves, migraines, chills, boils, joint pains, incontinence, swelling, insomnia, melancholia, and fatigue. She spent the majority of the postassassination years traveling to various health spas in America and across Europe seeking relief. During her final years, Mary lost most of her eyesight and had difficulty walking. It has been theorized she died of untreated diabetes.[3]

My dear Mrs. Bradwell:

How much I regret to say to you that I am suffering for the last two days with a severe headache,[d] which the Doctor[e] just tells me may settle in my head if I do not remain very quiet. I rise out of bed to tell you—for it is quite a source of annoyance to me that I shall not be able to see you tomorrow; but you may be sure, dear Mrs. Bradwell, that so soon as I shall be able I will call for you to claim you for a few hours.

You cannot begin to know what a treat it is for me to hear you converse and be near you. The doctor objects to my calling to see dear Mrs. Swisshelm[f] at present lest it may renew my nervousness in recalling past and far happier times. Before the week closes we will surely meet.

Most affectionately your friend,
Mary Lincoln[5]

A year passed in which the bond between Mrs. Lincoln and my grandparents was strengthened. Judge Bradwell had been Mrs. Lincoln's attorney for some time, and all matters of legal procedure she brought to him.[g] In the spring of 1874 my grandmother, fatigued from her activities as editor of the *Chicago Legal News*, went to Mobile for rest and recuperation. On May 6, 1874, Mrs. Lincoln wrote her a solicitous letter.

My dear Mrs. Bradwell:

Your kind note from Mobile was received several days since and I would have sent you an earlier reply had it not been for quite a severe attack of illness and this is the first day that I am out of bed for five days. Such terrible weather as we have had! I am delighted that you are enjoying yourself so very much and trust that you will return to us with your health entirely restored. Today is lovely here and I am even anticipating the Dr.'s[h] afternoon call with his sugar pellets and harmless draughts as a pleasant variety to the monotony of the day.[i] Our good friend, Mrs. Swisshelm has been confined to the house with severe quinsy[j] and you may be sure that

d. Mary suffered from migraine headaches her entire life.

e. It is unknown who this doctor is; Mary Lincoln had many. In a July 18, 1871, article, the *Chicago Times* named Charles Gilman Smith as her doctor, but Willis Danforth later testified at Mary's insanity trial that he began treating her in November 1873.

f. Jane Grey Swisshelm was an antislavery advocate, newspaper editor, lecturer, crusader, feminist, and Civil War nurse. She met Mary Lincoln at a White House reception in 1863.[4]

g. The earliest known legal act by James Bradwell for Mary Lincoln was when he examined the lease on her Chicago house in 1867. He also drew up her will in 1872.[6]

h. Dr. Willis Danforth

i. Mary's mention of her medications here as "sugar pellets and harmless draughts" is especially significant because her level of medication and how it may or may not have affected her mentality long has been a heated debate by historians. Some writers have theorized that Mary had no mental illness but rather was suffering hallucinations or delusions in 1875 due to overuse of drugs such as chloral hydrate. There is very little historical evidence concerning Mary Lincoln's medications. In a letter to Danforth, Mary asked him for "more powders," but she does not state what the powder is; Mary's sister Elizabeth Edwards said Mary was overindulging in chloral hydrate; and Mary's maid in a Chicago hotel said she saw Mary mix and drink medications, but she does not say what the drugs were. Dr. Danforth was a homeopathic physician who believed in the extreme dilution of medicines with water to increase therapeutic potency, so anything he gave her would have been mild to practically innocuous.[7]

j. An acute inflammation of the tonsils.

I am missing her greatly. Her quaint style is perfectly charming to me and such a relief to me from my *remembrance* of the artificial world, with which in former and *so much* happier days I was constantly surrounded. This note I fear will scarcely reach—ere you are leaving for C. (Chicago)[k]

With a world of love, believe me, your devoted friend.

Mary Lincoln[8]

Again that note of resignation! Mary Todd, who had dictated to the society of her day, anticipating the professional call of a doctor as a social adventure! It does seem to be evident, however, that she was able to take, superficially at least, more enjoyment in the everyday occurrences of life. But deep within still lurked the memories of her great sorrows, and the troubles of others seemed to recall poignantly the tragedies in her own life.

Nearly a year later Mrs. Lincoln wrote my grandmother from St. Augustine, Florida, where she had gone to escape the rigorous winters of Chicago.

St. Augustine, Fla.
Feb. 20, 1875

My dear Mrs. Bradwell:

Your kind letter was received some time since and although I have not replied to it believe me truly that you are frequently in my thoughts. And, I have so often wished that we could be together in this "Sunny clime." I am now looking down upon a yard with its roses, white lilacs and other flowers. (Although it is raining and we have had a good deal of rain in its soft, dreamy, light fashion,) since the middle of January, I remained too much out, on my balcony, took a severe cold, had much inward and outward fever for three weeks and one day when it was raging at its height I told my nurse[l] to pack up a small trunk and valise and we would leave town. So, on the 11th of Feb. we started for this place five hours distant from Jacksonville by boat and railway. On board the

k. Pritchard's editorial interpolations appear in parentheses, whereas mine are in square brackets.

l. Ellen Fitzgerald, the mother of acclaimed Vaudeville actor Eddie Foy, was hired by Robert Lincoln to be Mary Lincoln's "nurse, guard and companion" from 1872 to 1875. Foy later wrote, "Mrs. Lincoln had always been a woman of rather unusual disposition, and it will be remembered that she had had some spells of 'temperament' even while she was in the White House. After her husband's assassination she fell into deep melancholy, and after her son Tad died in Chicago in 1871 (the third son she had lost) she suffered from periods of mild insanity. She had many strange delusions at these times. She thought gas was an invention of the devil, and would have nothing but candles in her room. At other times she insisted on the shades being drawn and the room kept perfectly dark. Mother was with her at [Chicago] most of the time, but made one or two southern trips with her in winter. The position was a trying one, and Mother gave it up twice, but each time the kinsmen induced her to come back after she had had a short rest."[9]

steamer I met three or four choice Philadelphia friends, ladies and gentlemen and they insisted upon my joining them and instead of a modest journey of five hours to St. A. (Augustine) it proved four days and nights on the boat. If these *comme il faut* persons from the north generally and the most charming scenery on the celebrated Ochlawahs river could give pleasure, then it certainly was mine. Words would fail in description going from the broad St. John's into the narrow streams. With scenery such as is seldom met with in this world such pens as [poet William Cullen] Bryant and others have given minute details of the voyage. *Scribner's* November monthly speaks of it and Harper dwells at great length upon it. How much we will have to say to each other when we meet. From this most unexpected excursion I came here. I have been here five days, three of which have been passed in bed. For you may be well assured that the fever in my veins, must run its course. But two bright days I have emerged from it wandering over this quaint and most interesting place. My first visit was of course to the ancient Fort[m] and my wondering head was in every prison nook until we came to the one whose entrance was excavated I believe, in 1835, where two iron cages were found, one, now said to be in the Smithsonian Institute at Wash. hooked to the wall, where history records, and the Sergeant repeats, the story that two prisoners were enclosed in these same cages walled in, left to their fate, with God alone to be merciful to them! The prison of course is in darkness except the dim light held by the sergeant. I entered the fearful place and how I came out of it and how I have suffered in mind since our merciful Heavenly Father alone knows the wrongs of time will be redressed in a brighter world! My son[n] writes me that the winter has been terribly cold and my good friend and your dear husband, how is he getting along and how is his health this winter? What would I not give to see you again. My pen *as you perceive*, refuses its office.

With much love to you and yours
believe me, most affectionately yours,
Mary Lincoln[10]

m. Castillo de San Marcos, which Spain began constructing in October 1672. Upon the American acquisition of Florida in 1821, the name was changed to Fort Marion, in honor of General Francis Marion, the "Swamp Fox" of Revolutionary War fame. It was used mostly as a military prison.

n. Robert T. Lincoln in Chicago, Illinois.

Interior of Fort Marion, Fla., about 1890, with four female visitors standing on the parapet. Photo courtesy Library of Congress, Prints and Photographs Division, call number: LC-D4-3568.

Surely this letter was not written by a disordered mind! Yet, three months after she wrote it she was declared insane by a jury of prominent Chicago citizens and confined in a private lunatic asylum!

To those who knew and loved Mary Lincoln her conviction and incarceration as an insane person were gestures of an adverse fate so hideous as to be almost unbelievable. They held that there were friends and relatives whose doors stood open to her, whose protection she might have had, but those refuges were denied her because the courts had been appealed to and she was under their grim protection.[o]

And that appeal to the law was made by her own son, Robert Todd Lincoln!

There always has been considerable mystery concerning Mary Lincoln's insanity. Due to respect for Lincoln's memory, no doubt, the entire subject was given as little prominence as possible.[p] As an added precaution against undue discussion the court records were impounded, and it is due entirely to the courtesy and interest of Judge Henry Horner of the Chicago Probate Court that I am able to present them here.[q]

When Judge Horner examined the Lincoln letters and realized their import he readily consented to my consulting the court documents. He agreed that Mary Lincoln's correspondence with my grandparents would have an unquestioned bearing on the phases of history in which she played a part and, for that reason, should be accompanied by the official record.

That record discloses many interesting facts, not the least of which is that Robert T. Lincoln's application to try the question of his mother's sanity, the writ of inquisition ordering her arrest, the verdict of the jury finding her insane, and Robert Lincoln's petition to be appointed conservator of her estate all bear the same date, May 19, 1875.[14]

Robert Lincoln's petition to Judge M. R. M. Wallace of the Cook County Court sets forth that he would "respectfully represent that his mother, Mary Lincoln, widow of Abraham Lincoln, deceased, is insane, and that it would be for her benefit and for the safety of the community that she should be confined in the Cook County Hospital or the Illinois State Hospital for the Insane."[15]

As witnesses he named Dr. Ralph N. Isham, Dr. Willis Danforth, Samuel M. Turner, Maggie Gavin, J. R. Albertson, E. S. Isham, James P. Stone,

o. Unfortunately, this statement is untrue. Mary had alienated nearly all her family and friends while First Lady. By 1875 she spoke only to her cousins John Todd Stuart and Elizabeth Grimsley, and her closest friends Sally Orne and the Bradwells. Robert Lincoln did not ask for help with his mother, however, because he felt it was his duty to care for her, not someone else's. He also consulted seven medical experts who told him his mother needed professional treatment in a hospital. Pritchard's statement here seems to stem from Elizabeth Edwards's letter to Myra Bradwell of Aug. 3, 1875, in which she wrote, "Had I been consulted, I would have remonstrated earnestly against the step taken." Yet when Myra Bradwell asked Elizabeth to take Mary into her home, Elizabeth refused. She explained to Robert, "I am unwilling to urge any steps, or assume any responsibility, in her case. My present feeble health, causing such nervous prostration, as would render me, a most unfit person, to control an unsound mind."[11]

p. Untrue. Mary Lincoln's insanity trial was page-one national news when it occurred, and updates on her condition were regularly published during the ensuing year. Pritchard may mean that Mary's insanity was avoided in *articles* and *books* about her in future years, which certainly was the case until William E. Barton dug out the original court records in the early 1920s.[12]

q. This is true, but they were not impounded by Judge Horner until after Barton's *Life of Abraham Lincoln* was published in 1925. When Barton found the court records after an extensive search, they "had every appearance of not having been disturbed for many years," he recounted. Horner's action was taken out of a fear that making the papers public "might embarrass some members of Mrs. Lincoln's family who are still alive," meaning Robert Lincoln. Horner did make photostatic copies of the records and gave sets to the president of the Chicago Historical Society, the executive secretary of the Abraham Lincoln Association, and William Barton. No photostats were found in Pritchard's papers; she may have only borrowed a set from Horner.[13]

E. L. Dropp, T. C. Matlack, P. J. Maloney, J. S. Townsend, Nathan S. Davis, Hosmer A. Johnson, R. J. Patterson, J. S. Jewell, and Charles G. Smith.[r]

Although Dr. Barton, in his book, alludes to the existence of a transcript of evidence, there was none to be found nor did Judge Horner know when or how it had disappeared.[s] However, I was able to obtain much of the direct testimony from the *Chicago Tribune* of Thursday, May 20, 1875.[18]

Dr. Danforth, the first witness called, declared he had treated Mrs. Lincoln in November 1873 and again in September 1874 for "fever and nervous derangement of the head."

Dr. Ralph N. Isham, a close relative of E[dward] S. Isham, Robert Lincoln's law partner, the physician designated by Mr. Lincoln to give the principal medical testimony, submitted the following affidavit:

> I hereby certify that I have examined Mrs. Mary Lincoln, widow, and that I am of the opinion that she is insane and a fit subject for hospital treatment.
>
> Ralph N. Isham, M. D.[19]

Robert T. Lincoln told of many incoherent telegrams his mother had sent him from Florida and described how she insisted upon appearing before him partly clothed and in a distracted condition.[t] His testimony, however, chiefly concerned itself with her expenditures.

He said she had purchased $600 worth of lace curtains for her West Washington Boulevard home and had bought jewelry, including three watches, valued at $1,150. He gave much other evidence concerning the money she spent and urged these expenditures as proof of Mary Lincoln's insanity.[u]

Samuel M. Turner, manager of the Grand Pacific Hotel, where Mrs. Lincoln lived, Maggie Gavin, a chambermaid, John Fitzhenry, a waiter and Charles Dodge, cashier of the hotel, all testified that Mrs. Lincoln had behaved in a peculiar manner and that she continually complained of being followed by a strange man.

With this testimony the jury retired.

During the entire proceeding Mrs. Lincoln was calm. She did not take the stand, nor was a single witness called in her behalf.[v] The *Chicago Tribune* said of her:

r. In all, a total of eighteen witnesses testified against Mary. Samuel M. Turner was manager of the Grand Pacific Hotel; Maggie Gavin was a hotel employee who took care of Mary's room and slept with the widow in her room for four weeks; J. R. Albertson was a salesman for Matson & Co. Jewelers; J. B. Stone was a salesman for Allen & Mackey who sold Mary three hundred dollars' worth of lace curtains; E. L. Dropp was a merchant; T. C. Matlack [also spelled Mattock and Matley in different newspapers] with Haskel Bros. sold Mary several trunks; J. S. Townsend worked at a jewelry store; nobody named P. J. Maloney is listed as a witness in any newspaper; Dr. Ralph N. Isham was Robert's family physician; Drs. Hosmer Allen Johnson and Charles Gilman Smith both had helped treat Tad Lincoln during his final illness in 1871, and Mary characterized them as "two excellent physicians"; Dr. Richard J. Patterson was one of the Midwest's leading mental health experts and the proprietor and superintendent of Bellevue Place sanitarium in Batavia, Ill.; Dr. Nathan Smith Davis was an expert on the nervous system, the lungs, and the connection between alcoholism and insanity, and is known as the "Father of the American Medical Association," which he founded in 1847, at age thirty, and later served as its president from 1864 to 1865; Dr. James Stewart Jewell was one of the country's foremost experts on mental and nervous diseases; Dr. Willis Danforth was a homeopathic surgeon and professor of surgery, president of the Chicago Academy of Medicine and the Illinois State Homeopathic Medical Society, and Mary's previous physician.[16]

s. Barton was incorrect; there never was a transcript.[17]

t. On March 12, 1875, Mary suddenly became convinced that Robert was deathly ill, and she would not be persuaded otherwise. She sent a telegram to Robert's law partner inquiring after her son's health, stating she would start for Chicago immediately; ninety minutes later she sent a second telegram, "My dearly beloved son Robert T. Lincoln rouse yourself and live for my sake all I have is yours from this hour. I am praying every moment for your life to be spared to your mother." Robert telegraphed the station manager to discretely inquire "if Mrs. Abraham Lincoln now at Jacksonville is in any trouble mentally or otherwise"; the manager responded that Mary appeared "nervous and somewhat excited," and that her nurse "thinks [she] should be at home as soon as possible." Meanwhile Mary telegraphed Robert again, "Start for Chicago this evening hope you are better today you will have money on my arrival." Shortly thereafter Mary boarded the first available train and headed to Chicago. Robert was so worried that he monitored his mother's condition along her entire journey by having telegraph station managers observe her behavior and report back to him at every stop.[20]

u. A grief-stricken Robert, looking pale and weepy-eyed, reportedly broke down crying twice while on the stand. "His face indicated the unpleasantness of the duty he was about to perform and his eyes were expressive of the

"During the absence of the jury Robert T. Lincoln approached his mother and extended his hand. She grasped it fondly remarking with a degree of emphasis, 'Robert, I did not think you would do this!'[w]

"She was next approached by Swett (Leonard Swett,[x] who, with B. F. Ayer, represented Robert Lincoln), who tried to persuade her that it was for her good that the action had been taken. She could not be persuaded to believe what was said but replied with promptness that she would try to endure her persecution."

The jury, comprising Dr. S. C. Blake, C. B. Farwell, C. M. Henderson, S. M. Moore, L. J. Gage, H. C. Durand, S. B. Parkhurst, William Stewart, D. R. Cameron, James A. Mason, J. McGregor Adams, and Thomas Cogswell, deliberated but briefly.[y] They found that Mary Lincoln was insane and a fit person to be sent to a state hospital.[z] She was immediately removed to the Grand Pacific Hotel under guard[aa] and the next day was escorted to R. J. Patterson's private sanitarium for the insane [Bellevue Place] at Batavia, Illinois.[27]

On June 14, 1875, Robert T. Lincoln was appointed his mother's conservator, and I quote the docket entry in full:

> This day came Robert T. Lincoln who has heretofore, to wit, on the 19th day of May A.D. 1875, filed in this court his petition for the appointment of a conservator of the estate of Mary Lincoln, who has been by the verdict of a jury in this court declared to be insane and incapable of managing and controlling her estate, and due proof of service and summons on the said Mary Lincoln as required by law commanding her to appear before this court on this day and show cause if any she has or can show why a conservator should not be appointed to manage and control her estate being filed herein as also proof of publication of notice of such application, and no one appearing on behalf of said Mary Lincoln and no cause being shown why the prayer of said petition should not be granted and it appearing to the court that the said Robert T. Lincoln is a son of said Mary Lincoln and is a suitable and competent person to be entrusted with the control and management of her estate.

grief he felt," one newspaper reported. During his testimony—which was about much more than simply his mother's spending habits—Robert said he had no idea why his mother thought he was sick in March, as he had not been sick in ten years. He did not want any money from her. He took a room next to hers in the hotel and slept there for weeks, often sleeping in the same room to comfort her. Around April 1, Mary became increasingly paranoid and agitated. That morning, she tried to go downstairs in the hotel elevator half-dressed. Robert called the elevator back and sought to induce Mary to return to her room, an interference she regarded as "impertinent." When she refused to leave the elevator, Robert, with the help of a hotel employee, "gently forced her out," to which she screamed, "You are going to murder me!" He saw his mother listen and talk to voices in the walls and floor, and testified to her intense delusions and paranoia about fire as well as her many purchases, which he deemed useless since she never wore anything but black. He also testified to consulting with family friends and medical experts about what should be done. His mother had always been exceedingly kind to him, but Robert said he had "no doubt" that his mother was insane. "She has been of unsound mind since the death of father; has been irresponsible for the past ten years." He regarded her as "eccentric and unmanageable," meeting with strange people, spending lavishly on useless items, and ignoring his advice. "She has long been a source of much anxiety to me," he said. This is quoted from the *Chicago Tribune*, but all the major Chicago newspapers—*Times*, *Inter Ocean*, *Post and Mail*, and *Journal*—agreed in their reporting of Robert's testimony.[21]

v. The preponderance of the evidence points to Mary's silence, and was reported as such in the *Chicago Tribune* and the *Chicago Inter Ocean*, and in a letter from Leonard Swett to David Davis, in which Swett wrote, "In the court room she never spoke." The *Chicago Times*, however, reported that Mary often consulted with her attorney during the trial, and at one point, when a witness called her insane, she audibly asked the judge if witnesses were allowed to offer such a judgment.[22]

w. The *Chicago Inter Ocean* reported that Mary more vehemently exclaimed, "O Robert, to think that my son would ever have done this!"[23]

x. Leonard Swett was one of the most respected trial lawyers in Illinois, and was a legal associate and close friend of Abraham Lincoln. After Lincoln's assassination, Swett became a trusted advisor and friend to Robert Lincoln. Swett played an intricate role in Mary Lincoln's insanity case, advising Robert and helping to secure the medical experts and witness testimony for the widow's trial. He also was the one who brought her to the courtroom.[24]

y. The jurors were many of Chicago's most successful, capable, and respected men: Charles B. Farwell, member of the U.S. House of Representatives;

On motion it is ordered by the court that the said Robert T. Lincoln be appointed conservator of the said Mary Lincoln upon filing his bond as such conservator in the penal sum of one hundred and fifty thousand dollars with good and sufficient security conditioned as the law directs.

Whereupon said Robert T. Lincoln presents his said bond duly Executed with Henry F. Eames and Edward S. Isham as his sureties, and the court having examined and approved said sureties it is ordered that said bond be received and approved and that letters on conservatorship be issued accordingly.

And it is further ordered that said conservator assume the care, custody, control and management of the estate of said Mary Lincoln under the direction of the statute and of this court.

(Signed) M. R. M. Wallace
Judge.[28]

In his inventory Robert Lincoln reported his mother's estate as consisting of: cash, $1,029.35. United States Bonds and Stocks, $58,000. His personal bond to cover the unpaid balance of a loan of $10,500 made April 6, 1874, $8,875. The current installment of her annuity of $3,000 granted by Act of Congress was reported as having been paid to Mrs. Lincoln. Personal property was listed in two items, one for $549.83 was catalogued as lace curtains, while a second item of $5,000 was charged to nine trunks and a tin box containing personal jewelry.

The total of the estate he gave as $73,454.18.[29]

We may leave the court scene in the drama of Mary Lincoln now, but we must return to it later, for, in the room where she had been declared insane, with many of the same characters present, she was legally restored to reason and the possession of her estate.

Lyman J. Gage, cashier of the Merchants Loan & Trust Company, and later treasury secretary under President William McKinley; S. C. Blake, physician and former Chicago city physician (and member of the Lincoln and Hamlin Club of Chicago); businessman J. McGregor Adams of Crerar, Adams & Co. railway supply firm; insurance agent S. M. Moore of S. M. Moore & Co.; grocer Henry C. Durand of Durands & Co.; wholesale boot and shoe dealer C. M. Henderson of C. M. Henderson & Co.; jeweler Thomas Cogswell of Cogswell, Weber & Co.; crockery and glassware merchant S. B. Parkhurst of Parkhurst & Co.; jobbing stationer and blank book manufacturer D. R. Cameron of Cameron, Amberg, Hoffman & Co.; foundryman James A. Mason; and wholesale grocer William Stewart of Stewart, Aldrich & Co. Their deliberations lasted for "ten minutes," according to the *Chicago Inter Ocean* and "but a few minutes" according to the *Chicago Tribune*. The *Chicago Times* did not give a duration of time.

z. Forty-six years after the trial, juror Lyman Gage told historian William E. Barton that while Mary Lincoln did not appear violently insane to the jury, it was clear that she "suffered from phobias and occasional insane delusions," such as her fear of fire and her manic purchasing. "There seemed no other course than for the jury to find the lady guilty as charged," Gage wrote. He also stated that after the trial, "the leading physician who testified against" Mary—probably Willis Danforth, judging from time on the stand—privately told him there was "no doubt whatever of the fact of her mental aberration. . . . that it was a case of dementia, or degeneration of the brain tissue," and that within two years, she would die from it.[25]

aa. Mary was escorted back to the hotel by her son Robert and Leonard Swett. They left a female guard inside Mary's room to prevent the widow from jumping out of the window (because of her delusion of fire), and two male guards—one of whom was a Pinkerton agent—stationed outside in the hallway. All three were specifically instructed not to let Mary leave "on any pretense," but also not to physically restrain her in any way. The next morning Mary Lincoln talked her way past all her guards and visited three separate drugstores in the neighborhood of her hotel. At each place she tried to purchase a mixture of laudanum and camphor in an attempt to commit suicide by poison. The astute druggist at Mary's first stop, who had read about her insanity trial in the newspaper, sent for Robert Lincoln and gave Mary a harmless mixture of camphor, water, and burnt sugar. He also followed the widow to the next two shops and told the druggists there not to sell her any chemicals. Robert Lincoln eventually came and took his mother back to her room.[26]

3

Women, even the most courageous women of culture and refinement, cannot adapt themselves to abrupt changes of position and fortune as readily as men. Not so much because they are afraid, nor because they are unwilling to accept the altered conditions of life—whether they be for the better or worse—but because they lack man's definite purpose.

We're altering this situation rapidly, but in the days of the Lincolns, it was particularly true. Life, for Mary Todd Lincoln, was a succession of sudden, drastic changes involving her position in society and her personal fortune.

At twenty-one she ran away to her sister's home.[a] Though she was ever impetuous, this freed her of even the lax parental restraint she had known for several years. There opened before her a life of freedom she was unaccustomed to, and she was quick to avail herself of it. She lived in comparative luxury, for there were servants and many little attentions which, she would have said, could not be dispensed with.

In this environment she married Abraham Lincoln and forsook the servants and the little attentions for a two-dollar-a-week tavern.[b] They bettered themselves slowly, painfully for, years later, she wrote her sister that she was "[s]itting in the kitchen, one foot on the cradle rocker, one hand stirring the stew-pot, while the other holds my pen."[3]

Think of it! Kitchen-work, cradles and stew-pots listed as paramount issues in the life of a woman who, not long thereafter, was to be "the First Lady of the Land!"

Next came the splendor of the White House for, despite the hatred and contempt of Washington society, there was glamour there for her and it had its effect.

3

a. Mary later remembered her childhood as "desolate," but to say she "ran away" from home is a misleading characterization, especially under today's connotation. By October 1839, twenty-year-old Mary was so weary of living and clashing with her stepmother that she sought escape in Springfield, Ill., by arranging to live in the home of her sister Elizabeth Edwards. Elizabeth had always been more of a mother figure than an older sibling to her younger sisters after their mother died in 1825, and her house became not only the escape but also the match-making place for the Todd girls. Through her position as a social leader, Elizabeth Edwards introduced sisters Mary, Frances, and Ann to the men they would eventually marry. Records show Mary had visited the Edwards's house as early as 1835. In that year she witnessed a land deed for her brother-in-law, Ninian W. Edwards, who was selling land.[1]

b. They actually paid four dollars per week. The Globe boardinghouse was not as paltry as some historians have suggested, and beginning married life there was not an embarrassment. In fact, two other members of the Todd family began their married lives there: John Todd Stuart, Mary's cousin and Lincoln's first law partner, in 1837, and Dr. William S. Wallace and Mary's sister Frances, in 1839. The Lincolns actually followed the Todd family precedent so much that they inhabited the Wallaces' vacated rooms.[2]

She left that to go into a hostile world, alone. A world that misunderstood and misrepresented her. She had little money, then, for Abraham Lincoln's estate had not been settled and her own financial affairs were hopelessly tangled.[c]

She returned to Springfield and Chicago—home to her, now—and attempted to pick up the old threads. She found them broken and hopelessly frayed. Money did not worry her, but the attitude she faced on every hand, did.[d] She had a few friends such as my grandparents, Judge Bradwell and his wife, Myra, and seemed to find comfort in their companionship.[e]

Myra Bradwell, America's first female lawyer. She was Mary Lincoln's close friend and the recipient of most of the letters Mary wrote from the insane asylum. Bradwell has been considered the person most responsible for securing Mary's release from Bellevue Place sanitarium. Library of Congress, LC-USZ62-21202

c. Abraham Lincoln's estate had amounted to about eighty-five thousand dollars, but it was mostly in real estate and bonds, and so the family had only the yearly interest off which to live. That interest amounted to only about fifteen hundred dollars yearly each for Mary and Robert, which was enough to live modestly, but nothing more. Tad, as a minor, received only enough to pay for his own expenses. Mary's own financial affairs consisted of huge debts as First Lady that she had kept secret from her husband. Estimates of her debt range from ten thousand dollars to seventy thousand, although the latter figure seems more likely.[4]

d. Untrue; her letters show money constituted the majority of her worries: where and how she would live, whether or not Congress would give her the remainder of her husband's four years' salary, and whether she would receive a pension from Congress. Robert Lincoln, in fact, considered his mother "on one subject not mentally responsible"—money. Mary was upset that the Congress and the American public seemed to have forsaken her while lavishing praise and gifts on others, especially Gen. Grant. "Roving Generals have elegant mansions, showered upon them, and the American people—leave the family of the Martyred President, to struggle as best they may!" Mary wrote in 1865. She referred to the custom of honoring war heroes by giving them homes. Grant had been presented with homes in Illinois, Philadelphia, and Washington, D.C.[5]

e. Mary Lincoln had few true friends to turn to when she left the White House, having alienated or turned away from most of her previous acquaintances while First Lady. Besides the Bradwells, Mary kept in contact with Sally Orne, Rhoda White, and Eliza Slataper in the years after 1865.

Then she was declared insane and barred from the world in a private sanitarium at Batavia, Illinois. How one ever could become accustomed to such a change staggers the imagination.

The public heard nothing of Mary Lincoln from May 20, 1875, the day she was incarcerated in Dr. R. J. Patterson's insane hospital, until July 9, when a correspondent from the *Chicago Post and Mail* obtained an interview with her at Batavia.[f]

I quote a part of his report:

> I was anxious to pay my respects to Mrs. Lincoln in person. She occupies a suite in front of the house on the second floor. The attendant sits in the small room which contains a single bed. The larger room is Mrs. Lincoln's sitting and bedroom. It is very plainly furnished, the same as it was prior to her coming; an ordinary three-ply carpet, of pleasant colors, harmoniously blended, a bureau, rocking chair, and lounge and a plain bedstead, with a very fine bed, about which she is quite particular.[g] Mrs. Lincoln was seated in an expectant attitude by the table as we entered the room; she at once arose, shook hands with me cordially, and begged me to be seated, and began at once to inquire after friends in the city. She was dressed in ordinary black, half worn, with white ruches edged with black, in the neck and sleeves; her dark hair, fast turning to gray was carelessly coiffed in a knot at the back with coronet braid. She looked worn and ill. . . . She spoke tenderly of Mr. Lincoln, once as, "my husband" and again as "the President." Recalled memories of Noah Brooks, then her husband's Assistant Secretary, with whom I had an old-time acquaintance, and remarked that he had been for ten years engaged on the *New York Tribune*.[h] Asked me with much earnestness if the murderer of Hon. Sharon Tyndale of Springfield had ever been discovered,[i] and then alluded very feelingly to her attachment to Judge Bradwell's family. As I arose to leave she took a handsome bouquet from a crystal vase on her table and asked me to accept it. As she shook hands with me at parting, I thought I could perceive in the diplomatic bow and smile a return of the old society manner, and

f. This solitude—even hermitage—was by Mary's own design. The historical records suggest she was not only generally depressed, but also humiliated at her situation. The Bellevue Place daily patient progress report states that during her first seven weeks at the sanitarium, Mary had absolutely refused to see any visitors except her son and even kept to her room when guests were in the house or on the grounds. Both Dr. Patterson and the *Post and Mail* reporter were surprised when Mary assented to the interview.[6]

g. Mary Lincoln's personal bed and bureau from her room, as well as other furniture from the sanitarium during Mary's time there, currently are on display at the Batavia Historical Society in Batavia, Ill. Bellevue Place sanitarium itself still stands on Jefferson Street in Batavia, although it now is used as a residential apartment building.

h. Brooks was a reporter for the *Sacramento* [Calif.] *Daily Union*. He served in Washington as the paper's war correspondent from December 1862 to April 1865. He was never Lincoln's assistant secretary. He was intended to replace John G. Nicolay as the president's private secretary in 1865, but never took office due to Lincoln's assassination. In 1871 Brooks moved to New York and became night editor for the *Tribune*, and in 1874 quit to join the staff of the *New York Times*, where he worked for ten years.[7]

i. Sharon Tyndale was a former Illinois secretary of state who was found murdered near his home on Adams Street in April 1871, apparently the result of a robbery gone awry. His murderer never was found.[8]

my heart was full for the woman who sat down, silent and alone in her solitary room, to keep imaginary company with Senators and ambassadors in the light of that gracious, kindly smile long since hidden beneath the coffin lid.[j]

Meantime my grandmother had not seen Mrs. Lincoln since the latter's incarceration at Batavia as it was generally understood that Dr. Patterson and Robert Lincoln preferred that no one visit her in order that she might reap all the possible benefits from rest and quiet.[k] Shortly after the article above was published in the *Post and Mail*, with so many rumors being circulated, Mrs. Bradwell decided to investigate the situation herself. She went to Batavia, and what occurred is interestingly told in the following newspaper clipping.

[Ed. Note: Pritchard mistakenly gets the timeline of this event incorrect. Myra Bradwell went to Batavia after the article appeared because Mary Lincoln sent her a letter on July 28 asking her to come. The newspaper article Pritchard quotes below which relates how Myra Bradwell was refused entrance to Bellevue Place to visit Mary Lincoln was published on Sept. 4, nearly *twelve weeks* later than Pritchard states. Within those twelve weeks, a maelstrom of activity had occurred, including multiple visits and public statements by the Bradwells, which eventually spurred Robert Lincoln and Dr. Patterson to bar them from Bellevue Place.]

The following communication has been reluctantly furnished us, after the most earnest solicitation, by a lady of this city, who has, for many years, been an intimate friend of Mrs. Lincoln. The writer did not think of such a thing as publishing the result of her visit to Batavia, and from this fact, together with the high social position she occupies, great weight will certainly be accorded the statements made, and Mrs. Lincoln's friends be induced to have her case reopened.—(Ed. Courier.)

Anything which concerns the widow of our late lamented President is of interest to your readers. I have concluded, therefore, to give you an account of a visit I paid to Batavia yesterday. But first let me say, that I had no object in view in making this visit except to *satisfy myself* in regard to Mrs. Lincoln's insanity, of

j. Pritchard in her quotation here very cunningly elided over a part of the article in which the reporter sees Mary Lincoln as something other than sane. The full quote reads, "She looked worn and ill *and her hands, ringless and uncared for, were never at rest. I could plainly see in her lusterless eyes and in the forced composure of her manner, evidences of a shattered mind. She was perfectly ladylike in manner, but rambling and diffuse in her conversation.* She alluded rationally, however, to the past, spoke tenderly of Mr. Lincoln, once as 'my husband' and again as 'the President' . . ."[9]

k. There is no evidence that this is true. As previously stated, the evidence actually shows that Mary avoided all visitors and communicated with no one. Patterson later said he had no qualms about her receiving visitors or writing letters, which is why he allowed the *Post and Mail* reporter to ask for the interview.[10]

which so many have of late expressed doubts. The morning was a beautiful one. In passing over the country on my way to Batavia I was delighted with its loveliness. Nature did indeed have on her most regal robes. In due season I arrived at my place of destination, took a carriage to the hotel, and after a good dinner, inquired of mine host the way to the insane retreat. The building where Mrs. Lincoln is confined is a large stone building, with nothing to detract from its general appearance, except the bars at the windows, which, though diamond-shape, are none the less *bars*.[l] The grounds around the house are beautiful, and are laid out quite artistically.[m] I looked anxiously around, hoping I might possibly see my friend, Mrs. L., for I had learned she could walk in the grounds at her own pleasure, and I knew well how fond she was of such strolls. But not a person did I see anywhere around.

I ascended the steps of the house and rang the bell. Almost immediately the door was opened by a portly, fine-looking gentleman. I said: "Is this Dr. Patterson?" He said: "It is." I then introduced myself, and was courteously invited into his office. I said: "Doctor, I have called to see Mrs. Lincoln; she is a dear friend of mine and I thought I would like to see her a few moments, with your permission. I had no sooner spoken Mrs. Lincoln's name than a cloud passed over the doctor's face, and an expression, which I can best describe as *flinty*, took the place of what before was agreeable.

"Madam," said he, "have you a line from her son, Mr. Robert Lincoln?"

"No, sir," I replied, "I didn't suppose that was necessary."

"Where are you from, madam?" was his next question.

"From Chicago."

"Well, madam," said he, "you cannot see her unless you have such a paper."

"Couldn't I see her, doctor, in the presence of her attendant, my only object in coming here is to see her?"

"Well, madam," said he, "she may be out in a few days and you can see her to your heart's content." I said, "Do you consider her

l. There were no bars on Mary Lincoln's windows, as will be explained in more detail in chapter 5. This accusation was a dramatic fallacy created by Myra Bradwell to generate outrage and garner sympathy for Mary Lincoln's situation.

m. A visiting Chicago reporter described the grounds as being "of great natural beauty, and they are cultivated with much care, being laid out in walks and flower beds, which are under constant tribute to the inmates who desire them; evergreens and other shade trees are planted at regular intervals, and a fine greenhouse is nearly completed which will have a capacity for 6,000 plants, and has already nearly a thousand winter roses budded. This will connect by steps and an ornamental porch, with the first hall, so that patients can visit the greenhouse under cover. Pleasant lawn seats, rustic chairs and croquet games for those who wish are added to the comfort for inmates." Bellevue Place advertising brochures described the grounds as twenty "private and quiet" acres of manicured lawns and large and shady trees that help provide "the most favorable conditions" for the success of the overall medical treatment. There was also forty thousand square feet of greenhouses with walks and chairs, "where patients may enjoy at leisure the sunshine and flowers. In this soft, summer warmth, cheered by the sweet beauty of budding roses, the nervous invalid quite forgets her chill of spirit within and the chill of winter without."[11]

worse, Doctor? I understood from your letters to the public that she was allowed to see her friends."

"Well, madam, she is no *better*—for meddlesome people come here to see her, calling themselves her friends, when in reality they come out of self-interest only."

I said, "Doctor, please, don't attribute such a motive to *me*. I assure you my visit is only out of pure kindness to Mrs. Lincoln."

He replied, "I did not refer to you, madam."

"Well, doctor, as you are not willing for me to see her, will you allow me to leave a note for her?"

"No, madam, there is no necessity for that; it would only disturb her mind, and while she is under my care, I will not permit her to be disturbed, either by visitors or letters."

"If she is only permitted to receive letters except from such, she is virtually a prisoner, is she not?"

"Madam, she is no *more* so than other patients I have under my care."

While this conversation was going on, he kept looking at his watch, a gentle hint, probably, that I was trespassing on his time. "Doctor, it is some little time before the train leaves[;] if agreeable, I will sit here till then, as it is not very pleasant sitting in the depot."

He hesitated a moment, and getting up, said, very graciously: "You can sit in here," and ushered me into what was, I suppose, the parlor of the establishment, leaving me there, and for the time I stayed I did not see him again, or any one else. It struck me as being rather strange, inasmuch as I had heard his patients had the freedom of the house, but this, clearly, must be an erroneous impression of a good-natured public, I have no hesitation in saying that, if it should be my fortune to be placed in such an asylum, with the feeling within me that my friends placed me there with the desire to be rid of the trouble or care of me, or for some other end in view, or if I really believed they placed me there fully thinking me insane, and I saw no way out, and that speedily, it would take but a few days to make a raving maniac of me. Surrounded by those whose reason is dethroned, kept a prisoner to all intents

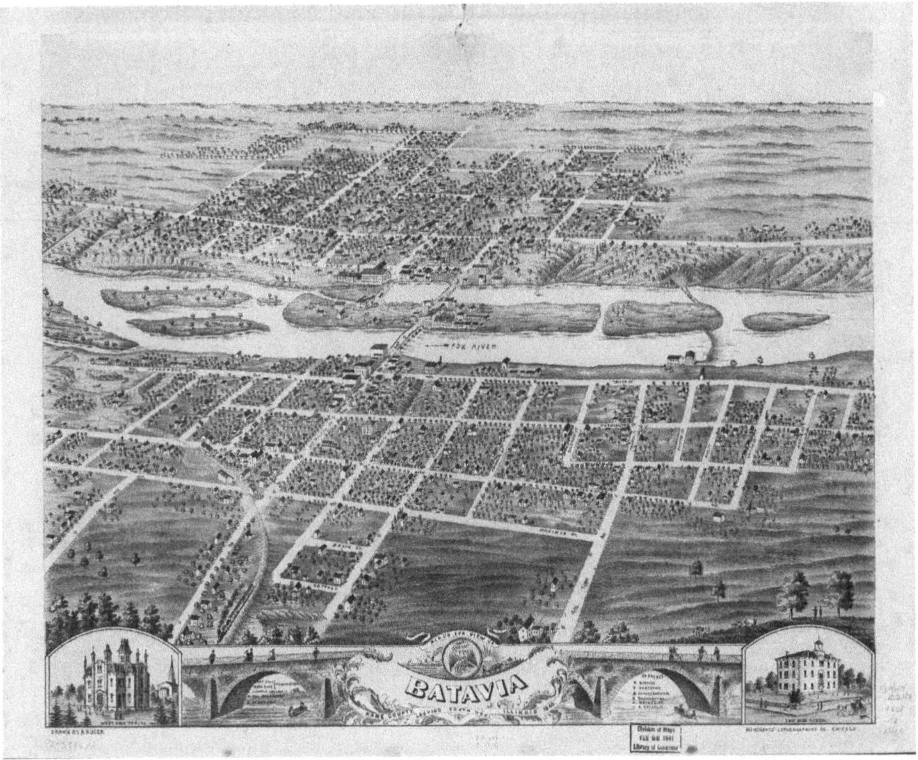

Map of Batavia, Illinois. Batavia, where Bellevue Place sanitarium was located, was a thriving town in a magnificent landscape. “You cannot imagine a cooler, shadier, more delightful retreat from the noise and heat of the city, than this beautiful little island town, with its charming surroundings, nestled cosily in the green hollow of the Fox River valley,” wrote a Chicago reporter who traveled to Batavia to visit Mary Lincoln in July 1875. “A lovely undulation of hill and dale threaded by a beautiful river, about whose borders a dense foliage casts lingering shadows. No picture on canvas can rival the landscapes I have seen here.” Robert Lincoln characterized Batavia succinctly as “the most beautiful country west of New York.”[12] While a patient at Bellevue Place, Mary Lincoln was allowed to take walks and carriage rides around the town—accompanied by an attendant—whenever she chose. The large building near the top left of the map with the number 3 above it is Bellevue Place sanitarium. Illustration courtesy Library of Congress, Geography and Map Division. Special thanks to historian Rodney Ross for revealing the existence of this map to me.

and purposes, having no voice as to who shall see me or call on me, being left to one particular party, and that party's interest perhaps antagonistic to mine; knowing that I was constantly watched and every move known; soon, very soon, should all interest in life cease, and if death did not end the darkness that moved over me, the seal of insanity would surely be written upon my brain, and all that remained of life would go out in that hour.

I must add that Mrs. Lincoln recently said she would gladly surrender her bonds for her liberty, as money would not replace that nor give back to her the affection of those for whom she would be glad to live and for whom she would gladly lay down her life.—Bloomington Courier.[13] [n]

Shortly after my grandmother's futile visit to Batavia, Mrs. Lincoln wrote to my grandfather and begged him to make the trip to see her. Already, I feel, she was hoping against hope that the few loyal friends left her would find some way of restoring her liberty. Following is the letter.

Wednesday, July 28th, 1875
Batavia, Ill.

My dear friend Judge Bradwell
May I request you to come out here just *so* soon as you receive this note. Please bring out your dear wife, Mrs. Wm. Sturgess,[o] and any other friend. Can you not be here tomorrow on the noon train? Also bring Mr. W. F. Storey[p] with you. I am sure you will not disappoint me. Drive up to the house also telegraph to Genl. Farnsworth[q] to meet you here. With much love to Mrs. Bradwell, believe me,

Truly yours,
Mary Lincoln

(Please pardon me if I mention that I will meet the expenses of your trip. M.L.)
In the event of Judge B. (Bradwell) not receiving this note in time, please come out on the afternoon train. M.L.[15]

n. It should be noted that when this article was published, Myra Bradwell's activism on Mary Lincoln's behalf had become a public spectacle; so when this article characterized her as a simple friend on a first visit to see Mary Lincoln with no intention of writing about it, other newspapers quickly exposed Myra Bradwell's ruse and harshly condemned it.[14]

o. William Sturges (Mary misspelled his name) was a Chicago banker whose wife, Carolina A. Sturges, worked with numerous women's charities in the city.

p. Wilbur F. Storey was editor of the *Chicago Times*, the most sensationalist newspaper in Chicago. During the Civil War, Storey was an antiwar Copperhead and the *Times* vehemently denounced the policies of the Lincoln administration, for which it was suppressed for a time by the government. For Mary to have turned to Storey for support at this time shows not only her determination in getting herself released from the asylum but also how well she understood the power of the press to sway public opinion.

q. John Franklin Farnsworth: Chicago attorney, Union Civil War general, and member of the U.S. House of Representatives in 1857–1861 and 1863–1873 (and had been present at Abraham Lincoln's deathbed in 1865).

Evidently this time both Judge and Mrs. Bradwell were enabled to see Mrs. Lincoln, and she must have begged them to write her friends in her behalf, for two days later, on July 30, 1876, Judge Bradwell wrote the Honorable John T. Stuart (a cousin of Mrs. Lincoln's) and Mrs. Bradwell wrote Mrs. Ninian Edwards, with whom Mary Lincoln had made her home in her girlhood days.

Below are the letters:

CHICAGO LEGAL NEWS COMPANY,
151 & 153 Fifth Ave.

Chicago, July 30, 1875
Hon. John T. Stuart

Dear Sir,

I saw Mrs. Lincoln at Batavia on yesterday. She desired me to write to you and say that she very much wants to see you, and would like you to visit her as soon as you can as she feels lonesome and that the restraint of the place is unendurable. I believe a visit from you would do her good and I hope you may be able to make it.

Mrs. Lincoln's general health has greatly improved. She spoke of Mrs. Edwards in the kindest terms, and expressed the wish that she might visit her at Batavia and said that she would like to return to Springfield with her and make her a visit. I believe such a visit would result in good to Mrs. Lincoln, and do no one any harm. Dr. Patterson said of all the patients he ever had at the retreat, Mrs. Lincoln had given him the least trouble. I am,

Very truly yours,
James B. Bradwell[16]

Copy of letter sent Mrs. Edwards, Springfield, Ill.

CHICAGO LEGAL NEWS COMPANY
151 & 153 Fifth Ave.

Chicago, July 30, 1875
Mrs. Edwards.

James B. Bradwell, a well-known public figure with a distinguished career during the fifty years he lived in Chicago. He was a Cook County court judge (1860–68), a member of the Illinois House of Representatives (1873–77), and a leader in numerous organizations such as the Chicago and Illinois State Bar Associations. Photo reprinted from *Album of Genealogy and Biography, Cook County, Illinois* (Chicago: Calumet Book & Engraving Co., 1895), 134–35.

Dear Madam:

I have just returned from a visit to your dear sister, Mrs. Lincoln. She desires me to write to you asking you to come up and visit her and expresses a wish to return with you to Springfield. She feels her incarceration most terribly and desires to get out from behind the *grates and bars*. I cannot feel that it is necessary to keep her thus restrained. Perhaps I do not look at the matter rightly, but let this be my excuse—I love her most tenderly and feel sorry to see one heartache added to her already overburdened soul.

She has always spoken most tenderly of you and I do believe it would do her good to meet you and receive a sister's loving tenderness.[r] Pardon the liberty I have taken in addressing you and believe me, your sister's friend

Myra Bradwell[18]

Four days after my grandmother wrote Mrs. Edwards, she received a reply full of sympathy and concern, showing decidedly that Mrs. Edwards did not approve in the least of Mary Lincoln's confinement at Batavia.

Springfield, Aug. 3rd.
Mrs. Bradwell,

Dear Madam:

I hasten to reply to your kind note, relative to my unhappy sister. My heart rebelled at the thought of placing her in an asylum, believing that her sad case merely required the care of a protector, whose companionship, would be pleasant to her. Had I been consulted, I would have remonstrated earnestly against the step taken.[s] The judgment of others must now I presume, be silently acquiesced in, for a time in the hope, that ere long, her physical and mental condition will be improved by rest and medical treatment.

The sorrows that befell her in such rapid succession and *the one so* tragic was enough to shatter the nerves and confuse the intellect of the bravest mind and heart. I regret to say that I cannot

r. Mary's relationship with her older sister Elizabeth was intimate during the Springfield years, but grew strained and distant about halfway through the Civil War. In 1861 President Lincoln had appointed Elizabeth's husband, Ninian W. Edwards, a Democrat, as Commissary of Subsistence for Springfield, Illinois. The city's Republicans decried the appointment for the next two years, charging fraud, financial malfeasance, and even treason in Edwards's official actions. By 1863 the clamor and criticism was so loud and overwhelming that Lincoln transferred Edwards to Chicago and stripped him of most of his responsibilities. This incident, as well as a letter by Elizabeth's daughter containing unkind remarks about Mary Lincoln, caused the First Lady to affect an estrangement with her oldest sister for the next ten years.[17]

s. In an August 11 letter to Robert Lincoln, Elizabeth Edwards apologized for her letter to Mrs. Bradwell: "I made a mistake in expressing to her, my views, upon the subject, of the treatment, I supposed would have been most beneficial to your mother. After having all the facts from you, her position, and difficulties in your family, I do not see, that you could have pursued, any other course." She added, "The only atonement I can make for improper interference if what I have done, is thus construed, is to assure you, that in the future, you have nothing to fear, from my intrusiveness."[19]

just now visit Mrs. Lincoln, being prostrated from the effects of a recent surgical operation. But will at once write to her and soothe her burdened heart, if possible, with words of love and sympathy.

It is my opinion that she should be indulged in a desire to visit her friends as the surest means of restoring her to health and cheerfulness. Accept my thanks, for your interest in my sister, and the suggestions you have made me.

Yours truly,
Mrs. N. W. Edwards[20]

This letter is conclusive evidence that Mrs. Lincoln was not regarded as insane by her entire family.[t] Her own sister, with whom she visited frequently and at length, would have remonstrated had she been notified, yet she was given no opportunity to have a voice in the action that legally stripped Mary Lincoln of all standing in society.

t. Untrue. Elizabeth Edwards's letter to Myra Bradwell shows she did not object to the diagnosis, but simply to the propriety of putting Mary in an asylum. In fact, nine days later, Elizabeth told Robert Lincoln in a letter that she considered her sister a person of "an unsound mind." She continued, "The peculiarities of her whole life have been so marked and well understood by me, that I have not indulged the faintest hope, of a permanent cure. The painful excitement of the *past years*, only added to the malady, [letter missing piece here] . . . apparent to her family for years, before the saddest events, occurred."

The rest of Mary's family in Springfield also considered her insane. John Todd Stuart not only expressed that he had "no doubt" that Mary was insane, but added that "Cousin Lizzie Brown" and "all [Mary's] relatives" in Springfield had the same opinion. It was reported at the time of Mary's Old Clothes Scandal in 1867 that Mary's family and friends in Springfield believed "the most charitable construction that they can put upon her strange course is that she is insane."

Myra Bradwell—similar to Elizabeth Edwards—also told both Dr. Patterson and Robert Lincoln that she believed Mary Lincoln *was* insane but "doubted the propriety" of keeping her in a sanitarium.[21]

4

Perhaps it was a concept of imagination formed in the minds of a saddened people, or it may have been really true that in 1865 Spring did come early and bestow her gifts lavishly. It may have been ordained as a colorful gesture of nature in recompense for the dark shadow of grief that was to mantle the official city on the Potomac and the nations.

The fact remains that you will read of April in Washington being a month of beauty, soft, flowering beauty that seemed to signalize the new peace. In the afternoon of April 14, Mary Todd Lincoln asked the President if he wished to have any one accompany them on their usual drive.

"No, Mary," he said. "I prefer that we ride by ourselves today."

They took a long drive, remarking the beauty of the Judas trees. Were those red flowers, blossomed so early and so profusely a symbol? During the ride Lincoln talked. It had been many months since he had had such an opportunity to take up the old things with this little spitfire wife of his!

"We have had a hard time since we came to Washington," he said, "but the war is over, and with God's blessing, we may hope for four years of peace and happiness, and then we will go back to Illinois and live the rest of our lives in quiet."[a]

Abraham Lincoln never returned to Illinois. On the night of that Friday John Wilkes Booth put a bullet in his brain. But Mary Lincoln went back—years later—back to Springfield and Chicago—and Dr. R. J. Patterson's private hospital for the insane at Batavia, where she was placed by court order in 1875.

From there she carried on the correspondence with my grandfather Judge James B. Bradwell and his wife, Myra, a correspondence begun three years before while she resided in Chicago.

4

a. Mary later said that Lincoln intended to take the family to Europe and then to California to "see the prospects of the soldiers digging out gold to pay the national debt." Husband and wife considered whether to settle back in Springfield, Ill., or live in Chicago upon Lincoln's retirement from the White House. "During the drive he was so gay," Mary wrote in Nov. 1865, "that I said to him, laughingly, 'Dear Husband, you almost startle me by your great cheerfulness,' he replied, 'and well I may feel so, Mary, I consider *this* day, the war, has come to a close." William Herndon declared that Lincoln intended to return to Springfield and resume his law practice "as if nothing had ever happened."[1]

b. "Intolerable" is more a moral and emotional judgment rather than a physical description of Mary's incarceration. Mary had her own private suite of two rooms on the second floor, including a private bath, in the part of the house reserved as the Pattersons' private residence. The larger room was Mary's sitting room and bedroom. The smaller room of Mary's suite was occupied by a personal attendant, a young former schoolteacher, selected for the position "on account of her kindness and intelligence." Mary's door was locked only at night, with the key kept by her personal attendant, who slept in the second room of Mary's suite. During the day Mary kept her room key and could walk or drive anywhere she chose on or off the grounds, while accompanied by an appropriate attendant, usually her personal attendant. She was allowed to receive visitors and to visit friends in the nearby town of Batavia. Mary often visited the Patterson family in their personal rooms on the first floor, sometimes taking her meals with them, the rest of the time eating in her room. "No other patient received such favored consideration," historian Rodney Ross has concluded. During her first two months in the sanitarium, Mary was quiet and docile, and, although depressed, clearly improving. Robert wrote to his mother's friend shortly after the trial, "My consolation in this sad affair is in thinking that she herself is happier in every way, in her freedom from care and excitement, than she has been in ten years." For the first month, Robert found his mother quite friendly to

She was incarcerated in May, and by late summer her confinement began to be intolerable.[b] She felt she could stand it no longer and the pent-up emotions of months demanded some outlet. Her letters became hysterical, and who can wonder at it? What person who has had the strain of waiting and hoping and praying for some great deliverance can not understand the reaction of this high-strung woman broken by a life of tragedies? Strange indeed she did not become a raving maniac!

On August 3 she wrote,

Batavia, Illinois,

My Dear Mrs. Bradwell:

Last evening I received your two most welcome letters. It is impossible to express the delight they afforded me and yet my disappointment is great that you do not propose coming out here until Friday. Your short stay prevented my doing what I had proposed or rather what I had mentioned to you.[c] Please write a letter to Mrs. Robert Anderson of St. Louis,[d] also Mrs. Judge May[e] I most *earnestly* entreat you, my very kind friend to come out on *Friday morning*, fail not, I beg of you.

It does not appear that God is good, to have placed me here. I endeavor to read my Bible and offer up my petitions three times a day. But my afflicted heart fails me and my voice often falters in prayer. I have worshipped my son and no unpleasant word ever passed between us, yet I cannot understand why I should have been brought out here.

I must see some of my friends and your noble, kind-hearted husband will see to this, I am sure, immediately. May I trouble you to write a letter to *Mrs.* Henry T. Blow[f] with a request that it will be forwarded to her in the event of her absence from St. Louis.

Mrs. Bradwell, my dearest friend, I love you very much. Go to my friends, go and see Mrs. Harriet Farlin[g] and her son Mr. Farlin, a partner of a Mr. Wing, real estate agents. Go To Mrs. F., she resides at 505 Michigan Avenue. Write a note when you receive him. "While she will not in words admit that she is not sane, still her entire acquiescence in absolutely everything, while it arises in part from the plain enfeebled condition of her mind, makes me think that she is aware of the necessity of what has been done," he wrote in early June. The Bellevue Place "Daily Patient Progress Reports" do show that by early July, Mary was growing restless. She started waking multiple times in the night, and on July 5 had a fit of crying. It was not until the Bradwells began their visits in late July—due of course to Mary's own solicitation—that Mary began to find Bellevue Place inhospitable.[2]

c. The meaning of this cryptic statement is unknown.

d. The Lincolns were friends with the family of Maj. Robert Anderson, the commanding officer at Fort Sumter at the beginning of the Civil War.

e. Unknown.

f. Minerva Grimsley Blow. Her husband, Henry Taylor Blow, served as President Lincoln's minister to Venezuela from June 1861 to February 1862, and then as a Republican Congressman from St. Louis, Mo., from March 1863 to March 1867. Blow's father, Peter Blow, had once owned the slave Dred Scott, whose lawsuit for his freedom in 1847 became the famous U.S. Supreme Court decision of *Dred Scott v. Sandford* in 1857. Mary Lincoln obviously was unaware of the death of Minerva Blow in June 1875, two months prior to this letter.

g. Mrs. Farlin stayed with Mary Lincoln in Chicago after Tad's death in July 1871 to offer support and commiseration.[3]

this to Gen'l Farnsworth requesting him to come and see me on tomorrow afternoon at four o'clock.

Pray for me that I may be able to leave such a place as this. Let me see Judge Bradwell. I beg you to come on *Friday morning.* I should like to see *Dr. Evarts.*[h] I feel that I must have some further conversation with him. Write me, your heartbroken friend, frequently, *daily.* But come to me. Will you kindly bring me out some samples of black alpaca a best quality without luster and without cotton. Also some samples of heavier black woolen goods.

Mary Lincoln[4]

In this letter and the one which follows, mailed a few days later, Mrs. Lincoln gives the first expressions of her growing resentment against her son, Robert Todd Lincoln, whom she begins to hold responsible for her confinement. I have been told that her repeated requests to have the people she names communicated with was a distracted attempt on her part to rally her few remaining friends about her that she might procure her release.[i]

A second letter in which she connects her son with her condition reads,

Batavia,
Wednesday, Aug.

My dear Mrs. Bradwell:

Your letter was received on yesterday. You did not state in what manner your Sabbath was passed. I am sure it was in a profitable way. I shall certainly trust to hear from you very soon, and without doubt, you will not forget me. God will not fail to reward you if you do not *fail* to visit the widow of Abraham Lincoln in her solitude. Does not Judge Bradwell's business bring him to the country *this* week and surely you will accompany him. Do not fail in coming to me when you receive this letter. Dear friend, as you love your Heavenly Father, come to me, bring your husband, the best of men. See Mrs. Farlin and Mrs. Davis her daughter. Please

h. Possibly Rev. Dr. W. W. Evarts, pastor of the First Baptist Church in Chicago. Evarts was a feminist who was connected to the Old Ladies Home and the Erring Women's Refuge in Chicago. He may have known Mary through her friends William Sturges and Presbyterian minister David Swing.

i. During this period, Henry T. Blow, whose wife (then deceased) Mary Lincoln had named in her previous letter, wrote to Robert Lincoln informing him of the letter he received from Mary through the Bradwells asking for assistance. Although the majority of Robert Lincoln's five-page response is illegible, the final two paragraphs state, "I suppose her letter to you was written with the hope of your aid to free her from the [illegible] nominal restraint she is now under. I think if you saw her you would approve my course. My responsibility is great and I cannot shirk it and I would be very glad to have the benefit of your advice. If you should come to Chicago at any time I should be glad if you could visit my mother. [illegible] . . . to see you and it might be that your visit would be productive of good to her. Please excuse the length of this reply. It is called for by your sympathy for my mother's unhappy state and I am very grateful to you."[5] There is no known evidence that Blow visited Mary Lincoln at Bellevue Place, wrote any letters to her, or made any response to Robert Lincoln.

write at once to my sister, Mrs. N. W. Edwards to come out here to see me. Explain everything. And if I have used excited words in reference to my son, may God forgive me, and may *you both* forget it. *Come*, come, is the watchword. You will when you receive this. Write to my sister. She is a sweet, intelligent, loving woman. And *Mrs. Blow* is nobleness itself. Write and do not forget my pleading. With kindest love to your husband and children, believe me,

Most affectionately yours,
Mary Lincoln.[6]

Say nothing to these people or any one else about the alpaca—you will understand.

Her parting admonition to tell no one of the request in a previous letter for alpaca would seem to indicate that she was forbidden to receive any articles of clothing other than those provided by the sanitarium.[j]

Mary Lincoln addressed her next letter to my grandfather, and its comparatively tranquil tone would indicate that my grandparents had informed her by letter of their purpose to do everything in their power to speed her release. That letter, dated August 8, follows:

My dear friend Judge Bradwell:

Knowing well your great nobleness of heart, I can but be well assured that you will soon see that I am released from this place. Mrs. Bradwell will explain everything. I am sleeping very finely and as I am perfectly sane, I do not desire to become insane. I pray you to see that justice is done immediately to me for my mind is entirely clear and my health is perfectly good. With a high appreciation of yourself and your wife, son and daughter, whom I love very much, believe me,

Very truly,
Your friend
Mary Lincoln[k]

August 8th, 1875

j. Untrue. Mary took numerous trunks of clothing with her to Bellevue Place, and she was allowed to order clothing and materials through the mails and to travel to nearby towns to shop. Her desire for Mrs. Bradwell to bring items is evidence of Mary's continued mania. Her desire for secrecy shows she knew her spending was considered one of her symptoms—whether she agreed with that diagnosis or not. One week after this letter, Robert Lincoln wryly noted in a letter to his aunt, "How completely recovered my mother really is is shown by Mrs. B[radwell]'s saying she was to take out to her samples of dress goods she wants to buy. She has with her *seven* trunks of clothing and there are stored here *nine* more."[7]

k. This letter is perceptibly different from all of Mary's other letters to the Bradwells. Where the rest are hastily written, rambling or erratic, and full of overt emotionalism, this one is clear, succinct, and cogent, written with a steady hand. Its utter restraint and professionalism, as well as the fact that it was addressed to James and not Myra Bradwell, suggests a deeper purpose than mere correspondence. In fact, this letter was written with such purposeful intent that it is not fanciful to call it almost a press release—it is easy to assume this letter to have been intended for inclusion in one of the many newspaper articles the Bradwells were promulgating at this time.[8]

Shortly afterward Mrs. Lincoln sent the following letter to my grandmother.

Batavia, Ill.
Friday, Aug. 1875.

My dear friend Mrs. Bradwell:

My son has just left me, after making me a short call. He mentions that he wrote on yesterday to my sister Mrs. N. W. Edwards of Springfield, requesting information of her, whether she would be willing to receive me as a visitor. I showed him her letter and he considered it a little cool and perhaps general. I rather think he *would* prefer *my* remaining *here* in his heart. *Myra* Bradwell write to my sister Mrs. E. (Edwards) *at once* the moment you receive this letter and beg and pray her as a Christian woman to write him R.T.L. (Robert T. Lincoln) urgently requesting a visit from him. A moment since Dr. P. (Patterson) returned from the drive to the depot and came to my door and announced that the Physician and Matron of the Elgin *Asylum*,[l] requested to be shown my room—and I am now expecting them every moment. I submit this to you both. Hoping and praying that the visit of tomorrow will not be *forgotten*. God in his mercy will not forget you. Also bring an exchange if you please, also that small key. Use your own judgment regarding the trunks. *When* we meet and I trust you will remember my desolation—much I shall tell you. It is necessary to see Judge Bradwell also. I wish I could kneel down for *one* hour; my heart faints within me. Write at once a most urgent letter to my sister, tell her to write urgently to R.T.L. My sister Mrs. C. M. Smith[m] has also written me begging me to come to her. Mrs. E. appears to be his specialty,[n] fail me not.

With much love
I remain truly yours,
Mary Lincoln.[10]

l. The Northern Illinois Hospital and Asylum for the Insane, established in Elgin (Kane County), Ill., in 1869.

m. Ann Todd Smith, Mary's younger sister, was the wife of Clark Moulton Smith, a Springfield, Ill., merchant. She and Mary had a falling out after Mary became First Lady, and during the war had a cold, even hostile, relationship. Apparently, Ann accused Mary of haughty condescension, as if she were a queen. In one letter Mary mentions Ann as having "a miserable disposition and so false a tongue. . . . and as a child and young girl, could not be outdone in falsehood." Mary's eagerness to visit Ann in 1875 indicates proof of the widow's desperation for aid and attention at this time.[9]

n. Reference to the close relationship between Robert Lincoln and his aunt Elizabeth Edwards; it also suggests a resentment against Robert for perhaps "preventing" Mary's visit to the Edwards home.

My grandmother visited Mrs. Lincoln the day the foregoing letter was written as her letter to Mrs. Edwards, which follows, indicates.

CHICAGO LEGAL NEWS COMPANY
151 & 153 Fifth Avenue,

Chicago, Aug. 11th, 1875.

Dear Mrs. Edwards:

I came in from Batavia last Saturday afternoon. Stayed with your sister Friday night. Slept with her and saw not one symptom of insanity.[o] She slept as sweetly and quietly as a kitten. Robert tells me if you will take her, he will bring her down to Springfield.[p] I do hope you will for she must be set at liberty. Do please take her and love her and I am sure you will not have any trouble with her for Dr. Patterson told Mr. Bradwell and myself that he never had a patient that made him so little trouble.

I am so sorry for the dear woman, shut up in that place. When they tell me she is not restrained, I want to ask how they should like it themselves?

I hope to hear from you soon,

Kindly, Myra Bradwell[13]

I have no definite knowledge of the exact steps to liberate Mrs. Lincoln taken at this time but I do know that my grandfather was doing everything in his power to have the case reopened.[q]

Not until many weary weeks later, however, did relief come and the period that ensued was rife with acrimonious debate, charges, and countercharges which, if they accomplished nothing else, did serve to bring Mary Lincoln's plight to the notice of the public and undoubtedly lessened the term of her captivity.

o. Myra stayed with Mary at Bellevue Place from Friday August 6 through Saturday August 7. On Friday Mrs. Bradwell had a "long discussion" with Dr. Patterson during which "she told the doctor distinctly that she had no doubt that Mrs. Lincoln was insane and had been for some time—but she doubted the propriety of keeping her in an asylum for the insane." The next morning Mrs. Bradwell told Dr. Patterson she believed her friend was "very much better." She also showed Dr. Patterson the August 3 letter she received from Elizabeth Edwards condemning Mary's commitment, told him to show it to Robert Lincoln, and suggested that Mary be allowed to leave the sanitarium and instead live at the Edwards home in Springfield, Illinois.[11]

p. Robert met with Myra Bradwell on August 10. "We had a long talk," Robert wrote his aunt Elizabeth Edwards, "the result which was that she thinks my mother is not entirely 'right' but that she ought to be at large. The only plan she suggested was her visiting you. I told her I do not object to that and we would await your letter." It is clear that Robert considered a proposed trip of his mother's to Springfield as a visit, while in her letter to Elizabeth Edwards, Myra Bradwell characterized it as a release and relocation from the asylum. "I told Mrs. Bradwell that the experiment of putting her entirely at liberty would be interesting to those who have no responsibility for the results. They can afterwards dismiss the matter with a shrug of the shoulders," Robert told his aunt.[12]

q. Bradwell in fact took no legal steps then or later, although he did threaten to do so. His and his wife's efforts were confined to fomenting public opinion. They wrote stories and gave interviews for the press, sent letters to Mary's family and friends that accused of harsh treatment and urged her release, visited and strategized with Mary, and continually accosted Dr. Patterson. This will be explained more in subsequent chapters.

5

Something within us prompts sympathy for the vagabonds, the wanderers. Because their feet continually stir strange dust, their eyes ever regard unaccustomed scenes, we give them our sympathy.

"These," we say, "are lost people. Aimlessly they tread roads that have no end; embark upon journeys that have no destination. How lost they are since theirs is a path through scenes that change with the days!"

There is pathos in the lives of such, and they are, to us, lost since they have forgotten whence they came and are not concerned with where they are going.

But can any living being be more hopelessly lost than the person in confinement? Can there be greater pathos than that which enters the lives of those who are imprisoned?

To look, day upon day, week after week at the same horizon, to see the same limb fall against the sky at the same angle, to know just how each bush and tree and building looks at mid-morning, at noon and at twilight, to know these things and to be unable to step beyond them, can life be more pathetic than that?

I do not think so, and because I do not I always have felt that Mary Todd Lincoln was lost, to the world and to herself, during the period she was incarcerated in Dr. R. J. Patterson's sanitarium for the insane at Batavia.

To be sure she had the freedom of the grounds at certain hours, but much of her time was spent within her room, where she sat gazing through a window—a barred window—longing for the freedom that always had meant so much to her.[a]

5

a. As previously stated, Mary Lincoln had complete freedom of the buildings and the grounds. Her windows were not barred. Every room in Bellevue Place had windows fitted with a protective covering to prevent falling. Dr. Patterson called it a "light ornamental screen;" Robert Lincoln referred to it as "a white wire netting such as you may see often to keep children from falling out of the window;" a female journalist who toured the hospital described it as "merely an ornamental screen of steel wire, with a six inch mesh, woven in a diamond pattern, not at all suggestive of bars." This covering was removed from Mary's room at Robert's request but was later reinstalled by Patterson after he remembered Mary's attempted suicide the day after her trial.[1]

Bellevue Place sanitarium in Batavia, Illinois, as it looked during Mary Lincoln's stay in 1875. Advertised as a "cheerful and homelike" retreat for the treatment of nervous and mental diseases, Bellevue Place admitted only high-class, nonviolent, female patients. Courtesy Batavia Historical Society

Summer had come, a riotously gay summer, but it brought no beauty, no languorous ease to Mary Lincoln. It merely added the element of heat to conditions already intolerable.[b]

About this time, rumors regarding her were being circulated once more, and the newspaper world awoke to the fact that she might soon be liberated.[3] A representative from the *Chicago Times* went to Batavia to see her, and I quote his report here.[c]

> The public was somewhat shocked a few months since by the announcement that Mrs. Lincoln, the widow of President Lincoln, was insane; and further pained by the announcement of the fact that she had been confined in a private insane asylum at Batavia, in this state, owned and managed by Dr. Patterson. The proceedings before the court were reported with great fidelity, and published in detail in the newspapers of the city. The account of her subsequent departure from the city, was also given to the world with a painful minuteness. Occasionally some word has come up to the great busy world from the retired spot of earth, concerning the condition of the lady in whom all American people feel a kindly interest. These slight allusions to her were eagerly read, then the active affairs of life went on, and no one thought of the woman who had suffered so much in this world, and whose afternoon of life is filled with such a chilly atmosphere.
>
> Recently a representative of THE TIMES, in quest of scientific facts by means of personal observation, visited the institution of Dr. Patterson at Batavia, and while there was
>
> INTRODUCED TO MRS. LINCOLN
>
> by a mutual friend who happened to be there at the same time,[d] not as a newspaper man but as a gentleman who knew her history and who took a friendly interest in all that pertained to her welfare.
>
> The lady appeared in very good spirits, and her mind was clear and sprightly. After some preliminary conversation she invited the gentleman to her room to obtain a view of the pastoral landscape from that source, and to pursue the interesting conversation already begun. This opportunity, which had thus been presented

b. The living situation at Bellevue Place sanitarium was far from intolerable. The main building was a massive, three-story limestone structure, complete with ivy creeping up its walls. The interior was bright and spacious, with hallways one hundred feet long and twelve feet wide, high ceilings, and large, well-lit rooms. The décor, with elegant furniture, potted plants, and vased flowers, was designed "as to give a bright, cheerful and homelike expression," so that "in all its appointments, [Bellevue] is intended to create an atmosphere of home, with its restfulness, freedom, and seclusion."[2]

c. This article was written by Franc B. Wilkie, principal writer (editorial and otherwise) for the *Chicago Times* newspaper. He was described in 1868 as a man of large imagination, who wrote with ease and rapidity, preferred sentiment to dry logic, and "hesitates at no subject." He visited Mary Lincoln on Saturday, Aug. 7, the fruition of Mary's July 28 letter to James Bradwell in which she asked him to bring *Times* editor Wilbur F. Storey to Bellevue Place. After spending the night of Friday, Aug. 6, in Mary's room, Myra Bradwell left Saturday morning for Chicago and returned at 1 P.M. with Wilkie. The three spent two hours in private conversation in Mary's room. At the time of his visit, Dr. Patterson was absent (actually visiting Robert Lincoln in Chicago) and none of the employees at the sanitarium knew who Wilkie was, although it did not take them long to find out. Patterson and Robert Lincoln were furious that Myra Bradwell had brought a man who was a complete stranger to them—and a journalist besides—to visit Mary. Their indignation was magnified by the fact that the visit purposely occurred on a Saturday, when both women knew Dr. Patterson would be away from the sanitarium. "I can but regard this as a breach of hospitality, and of common courtesy to me," Patterson wrote to Myra Bradwell the next day. He told her that she needed thereafter to get Robert Lincoln's approval for any future visits, especially if accompanied by a stranger, as well as for mailing or conveying any of Mary's letters. Robert called Myra "a pest and a nuisance," and "characterized her introduction of Mr. Wilkie . . . as an outrage." Wilkie's article was not published until Aug. 24.[4]

d. Myra Bradwell, who actually went to Chicago to fetch the reporter and bring him to Batavia specifically so he could write a story.

by circumstances, was improved by the gentleman of the press, to discover the exact condition of her mind, so far as he was able to do so, by drawing her into conversation on all possible topics in which he deemed her to have been interested, either pleasantly or painfully during her life. If there were any weak points in her mind, he was determined to find out what they were. If she were brooding over any circumstance of her sad life, he was bent on finding out what it was. Her visit to London was alluded to, and thoroughly discussed.[e] Little Tad was with her there, and she alluded to the child, now dead, but whose memory is very dear to her, with all the warmth and affection a fond mother might be expected to exhibit. There was, however,

NOT A SIGN OF WEAKNESS

or any abnormal manifestations of mind visible. She conversed fluently and rationally about her wanderings in England. She narrated her experiences in Germany, dwelling on the subject of her travels with much detail and interest to the end. During all this time she not only exhibited a sound and rational judgment, but gave evidences of the possession of uncommon powers of observation and memory.

Her attention was called to the time when the visitor had met her in Washington, in 1862. The occasion she remembered. Knowing that the death of little Tad and the assassination of Mr. Lincoln were two incidents in her life that were known to have made the most powerful impressions on her mind of any events which had ever occurred to her, these circumstances were adroitly introduced into the conversation. During all this her admirable mind maintained its poise with perfection. Concerning Mr. Lincoln she related anecdotes illustrating his extreme good nature. She conversed about the assassination. No mental weakness, under any possible test, could be discovered. She spoke of public men with whom she had become acquainted during her residence at the White House. She specially dwelt on the friendship which existed between Mr. Seward[f] and Mr. Lincoln and herself. It was the habit

e. Mary and Tad traveled throughout Europe from 1868 to 1871, residing mainly in Frankfurt, Germany. In November 1870, mother and son took rooms in Woburn Place, off Russell Square, in London. There, Tad resumed his schooling begun in Germany, while Mary was reportedly "well received" by Americans in the city. She visited with multiple American friends and acquaintances, including Colorado governor John Evans, U.S. consul general in London Adam Badeau, former minister to London John Lathrop Motley, and Alice D. (Mrs. Paul R.) Shipman, daughter of a childhood Kentucky friend. Mrs. Shipman later recalled, "I saw much of [Mary Lincoln] in London, where she and her son Tad with his tutor were wintering. I was confined to my couch and she was my frequent guest. Her conversation, always genial, was usually in the minor key."[5] Mary left Tad in school in London and went by herself to Florence, Italy, in early February 1871 to travel with friends. The Lincolns left England and returned to the U.S. in May 1871.

f. Mary was revising history here. Although Abraham Lincoln and Secretary of State William H. Seward were great friends, Mary was not a part of that friendship. Mary, in fact, did not trust Seward, never liked him, and could in no way be called his friend. She believed Seward thought himself superior to the president, and therefore was untrustworthy. "You will generally find it a safe rule to distrust a disappointed, ambitious politician," Mary once chided her husband over his faith in Seward's goodness. "It makes me mad to see you sit still and let that hypocrite, Seward, twine you round his finger as if you were a skein of thread." Mary never missed an opportunity to criticize the secretary of state, according to her White House dressmaker and confidante, Elizabeth Keckley.[6]

of the secretary to dine with Mr. Lincoln and herself informally, two or three times a week. She

ALLUDED TO THE MOTLEYS[g]

whom she met in England, and spoke with great sensibility of their kindness, and told how badly she felt when the minister was removed. She very keenly described the characters she had met abroad, showing that she possesses great powers of analysis. She gave her views of foreigners, and foreign matters, concerning which she exhibited great apprehension and acuteness of mind. She also spoke of the books she was engaged in reading and the life she led. Her health at present, she observed, was superb. She had never been better. When she came to Chicago from Florida she had been suffering somewhat from fever, and her nervous system was somewhat shattered. She was prostrated, and any eccentricities she might have manifested then, if any, she attributed to this fact.[h]

There were some light iron bars over the door, to which she called the attention of the gentleman. She said they seemed to menace her, and they annoyed her with the idea that she was in prison. She was somewhat apprehensive that the prison bars, and the presence of insane people in the house, whose wild and piercing cries she sometimes heard, might affect her mind so as to unseat her reason, in time.[i] She commented upon journals and journalists with great intelligence. The conversation took the widest possible range, and from this the representative of THE TIMES became convinced that her mind was in

A PERFECTLY SOUND AND HEALTHY CONDITION.

She made no complaint of her treatment. She thought she would like a little more liberty to drive out, and a little more liberty to receive her friends. She exhibited marvelous charity through the entire course of the interview for those by whose instrumentality she had been placed there. The gentleman departed thoroughly convinced that whatever condition of mind Mrs. Lincoln may have been in previously, she is unquestionably *compos mentis* now, and ought not to be deprived of her liberty.

g. John Lothrop Motley, U.S. minister to Great Britain, 1869–70, while Mary and Tad were touring Europe. President Lincoln appointed him minister to Austria in 1861, where he served until 1869.

h. Mary made this same statement to her sister, Elizabeth Edwards, who told it to Robert Lincoln. "Surely, the evidence of derangement exhibited last spring, must have arisen from physical disorder. She informs me that her health was poor before going to Florida, and during her stay there, and on her return, was often conscious, of the presence of fever—moreover, had used chloral very freely, for the purpose of inducing sleep. Those causes, had doubtless much to do, with producing the sad result," Edwards wrote.[7]

i. These statements of Mary were clearly for dramatic effect. Besides being no bars, there would have been no, or practically no, "wild and piercing cries." Bellevue Place admitted only the best of patients. Typical patients—all of whom were female—were nervous invalids who were not insane but "who occupy a border-land between undoubted insanity and doubtful sanity"; and incurable patients who either could not gain admission to state hospitals, or whose families preferred a more private retreat. The *Post and Mail* reporter described the other twenty inmates at Bellevue with Mary Lincoln as the wives of rich men, "the majority are melancholy—some are suicidal—all are quiet—the doctor preferring not to take noisy patients into his well-organized family."[8]

A reporter of THE TIMES last evening called on

MRS. MYRA BRADWELL

at her residence on Michigan Avenue, and obtained from that lady some interesting particulars concerning Mrs. Lincoln. Mrs. Bradwell has been a warm personal friend of Mrs. Lincoln for some years, and has been in active correspondence with her during the past year. She has been associated with her intimately, and is thoroughly acquainted with her mental condition. During the past few weeks this lady has visited Mrs. Lincoln at Batavia several times, and has conversed with her for hours. She has occupied the same room and the same bed with her, and has received letters from her full of sensibility, affection, and pathos.

"What have you to say concerning Mrs. Lincoln's condition, Mrs. Bradwell?" asked the reporter after disposing of the preliminaries to the subject.

"I am extremely reluctant about saying anything about the matter at the present time," replied the lady, "on account of the unpleasant situation of things."

R.—I am informed that you have visited Mrs. Lincoln several times recently, and have had long conversations with her?

Mrs. B.—So I have. I have always had the tenderest regard and love for Mrs. Lincoln, and during her stay in Florida received many long and beautifully written letters from her. I was inexpressibly shocked when I learned of her alleged insanity, and of her confinement in an asylum at Batavia. I wondered what could have occurred to unbalance her mind so suddenly. It was a matter of the greatest surprise and astonishment to me.

R.—Do you think Mrs. Lincoln is insane?

Mrs. B.—I will be frank with you in answering that question. I think Mrs. Lincoln has no more cause for being confined behind bolts and bars than any other person whose sanity is not questioned. She is no more insane than I am.

R.—What was the object of your visit to Batavia?

Mrs. B.—I felt a deep interest in the welfare of Mrs. Lincoln. I went to see her and conversed with her for two hours. I obtained

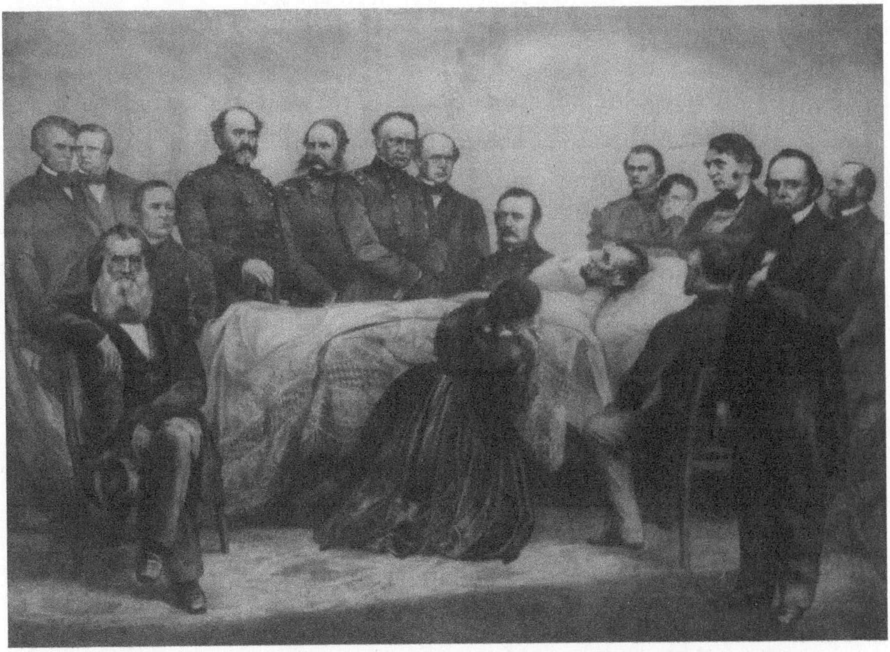

"Death Bed of Lincoln." Mary Lincoln's mental unbalance did not come on "suddenly," as Myra Bradwell told the *Chicago Times*, but had been building for years, probably her entire life. Most physicians, friends, acquaintances, and family of Mary Lincoln—including her son Robert—believed her "insanity" stemmed from the shock of her husband's assassination in 1865. PGA–Brett (A.) & Co.; courtesy Library of Congress.

permission of Dr. Patterson to visit her again. I went again and again.

The foregoing was the substance of the conversation with Mrs. Bradwell, who feels the keenest interest in the welfare of her friend. There seems to be no doubt that Mrs. Lincoln's mind is now sound and that she will be restored to the world in a short time.[j]

Editorially the *Times* said:

One of the saddest of all sad incidents connected with the life of Mrs. Abraham Lincoln was the recent proceeding by which her own son secured her incarceration in an insane asylum. When a woman spends *her own* money lavishly and appears a little different from others she ought not to be placed behind iron bars. If this sort of proceeding is to be countenanced where will the end be? Mrs. Lincoln has had enough trials and troubles to break down an ordinary woman, and yet she has borne all and wronged no one. Let her be released.[k]

Not long after the appearance of the report and the editorial I have quoted above, the *Chicago Post and Mail* sent a reporter to interview my grandfather, Judge Bradwell.[l] Because that interview has a direct bearing on the letters which occasioned this series of articles, I reprint it here. I think it does much to clarify my grandfather's position in the Mary Lincoln controversy, a controversy that was to become bitter and engender hatreds ere it found an end.

The interview follows:

A representative of THE POST AND MAIL called at the office of the *Legal News*, and soon found the courteous and humane Judge at leisure for an interview, though at first somewhat averse to it. Only the strong feeling of his good heart that Mrs. Lincoln was

A WRONGED WOMAN

and that, as a President's widow, the public were interested in her personal welfare, and had a right to know the facts, induced him to talk upon the lamentable theme.

j. Pritchard did not transcribe the entire newspaper article in her manuscript, possibly because some of Myra Bradwell's statements during her interview contradict Pritchard's thesis. Here is the remainder of the interview as printed:

R.—What did you do upon your return to Chicago, Mrs. Bradwell?

Mrs. B.—Upon my return to Chicago from my first visit I obtained an interview with Mr. Robert Lincoln. I told him what I thought of the condition of his mother, and I referred to my long acquaintance with her. He acknowledged to me that he thought I was acting for what I deemed the best interests of his mother. If Mrs. Edwards, of Springfield, a sister of Mrs. Lincoln, would receive her, he would go himself to Batavia and conduct her there, provided Dr. Patterson would sign a certificate of recovery.

R.—Has Dr. Patterson signed such a certificate?

Mrs. B.—He has, but it has not been delivered to Mrs. Lincoln.

R.—Did you learn whether Mrs. Edwards would receive her sister?

Mrs. B.—I did. I made a visit to Springfield. I had a long conversation with her. She promised to receive her sister and take care of her. Mrs. Edwards is a lady of fine feelings and cultivation. She has a beautiful home, surrounded by lawns and flowers. It is just the place for a sorrow-burdened heart like Mrs. Lincoln's to find repose and peace. On my return here I had called to see Mr. Robert Lincoln, but he had gone east. Nothing can be done until his return. It is this circumstance which causes me to regret the publication of anything concerning this matter at the present time. It is premature and places me in a delicate position. It would have been better to have delayed it.

R.—Do you think Mrs. Lincoln's release can be obtained without an appeal to the law?

Mrs. B.—Unquestionably. I have no reason in the world to doubt Mr. Robert Lincoln's word. I believe he will do as he said he would. He informed me though, that he was very certain Mrs. Edwards would not consent to receiving her.

R.—What did Mrs. Lincoln say about a visit to her sister?

Mrs. B.—She implored me in the tenderest and most pathetic terms to go and see Mrs. Edwards and ask her to receive her.

R.—How did you find her situated?

Mrs. B.—I found her very comfortably cared for. When I first went there, there were bars over her windows and doors and this fact seemed to annoy her. I spoke to Dr. Patterson about it, and the next time I visited her she was in a room without bars. The bolt was not turned on the outside, which afforded her some relief."

Myra Bradwell's statements in her interview contain many half-truths or outright fallacies. Dr. Patterson never signed a certificate of recovery

The following dialogue ensued:

Reporter—Judge Bradwell, is THE POST AND MAIL correct in inferring that yourself and Mrs. Bradwell are the legal gentleman and lady referred to by the correspondent as taking legal steps for the permanent release of Mrs. Lincoln from her confinement at Batavia?[11]

Judge Bradwell—Well, I don't know, as I didn't see your correspondent. She certainly learned nothing from me. I have been to see Mrs. Lincoln several times of late, as also has Mrs. Bradwell; but no strictly "legal" steps have been taken, as it is hoped that her release from

HER UNJUST INCARCERATION

can be effected amicably. Do you want to write anything about this?

R.—Certainly; if you know anything about Mrs. Lincoln's condition and confinement at Batavia which the world doesn't know, and are disposed to tell it, THE POST AND MAIL, as always, will be inclined to enlighten the world by the publication of your information.

J.B.—Well, sir, I have no hesitation whatever in saying that Mrs. Lincoln ought not to be where she now is, and never ought to have been placed there. It was

A GROSS OUTRAGE

to imprison her there in a place understood to be for mad people. Why to be so shut up and guarded and locked up at night, with the feeling that it may last for life, is enough to make almost any aged and delicate woman crazy. She is no more insane today than you and I are.

R.—What makes you think so, Judge?

J.B.—I am as

THOROUGHLY CONVINCED OF IT

as of my own existence. I have had several business letters from her since she has been there, and Mrs. Bradwell has had letters of womanly friendship from her repeatedly; and she writes as

for Mary Lincoln; Elizabeth Edwards had not consented to receive Mary Lincoln in her home at the time this article was published, although she did so later; Robert Lincoln never made any promises to Myra Bradwell concerning his mother's release, but by saying he did Bradwell put him in an awkward situation; and the "bars" on Mary's windows were removed at Robert's request, not Myra Bradwell's request.[9]

k. This is not from the *Chicago Times*, and neither the newspaper nor the publication date of Pritchard's quote could be determined. The *Times*'s editorial that day stated, "The public had read the harrowing tales of the imprisonment of sane men and women in asylums for the insane. Some of these were doubtless true, others fictions. That such things have been done does not admit of a doubt. The subject is brought forward again in a painful manner by an interview with Mrs. Myra Bradwell, editor of the *Legal News*, a lady of prominence and unquestioned veracity, who has several times visited Mrs. Lincoln at the retreat for the insane at Batavia, Illinois. Mrs. Bradwell is of the opinion, from a close study of the patient, that there is not the slightest trace of insanity about her. She thinks Mrs. Lincoln has been grossly abused, that she is today as sane as those who adjudged her otherwise, and should at once be restored to liberty and the control of her own affairs.

"The case is a peculiarly sad one. It will be remembered that the jury which adjudged Mrs. Lincoln insane was selected with extraordinary care; that the examination of witnesses was reasonably thorough, and that the evidence presented was sufficient to convince even the most reluctant of her friends, of Mrs. Lincoln's mental aberration. But if she has since recovered her right mind, and is being held in duress unlawfully, and without good cause, the public will unite in a demand for her release and restoration for her proper place in society."[10]

l. In fact, the interview was conducted and the article published *before* the *Times* story—evidence of the concerted and concocted publicity effort of the Bradwells.

straight and intelligible a business letter as she ever did, and as good, friendly letters as one need ask for. There is

NOT THE SLIGHTEST TRACE OF INSANITY

or of a weak mind about any of her writings.

R.—Well, a good letter is one of the best proofs possible of a sound mind. Will you permit one of more of her letters to be printed?

J.B.—I should hardly feel warranted in doing that without Mrs. Lincoln's consent; but you may take my word for it that they are good sane letters.

R.—When did you see and talk with her last?

J.B.—One week ago today.

R.—What did she say about herself?

J.B.—She sighed and pled for liberty like a woman shut up without cause. Said she to me: "Mr. Bradwell, what have I done that I should be kept here in this prison, behind these grates, my footsteps followed, and every action watched by day, and my bedroom door locked upon the outside at night, and the key taken away by my jailer? Sure 'I am not mad, but soon shall be.'

I WANT LIBERTY

to go among my friends."

R.—Is it not a pleasant place then?

J.B.—Oh, yes; the scenery is fine, and Mrs. Lincoln eats well and sleeps well, and has a healthy look. But she does not well brook the idea of being a prisoner. I sat in the room with her and looked out upon the Fox River with the forests and the flowers and the lawn, and said to her: "Mrs. Lincoln, this is very nice." She replied: "Yes, it is very nice to you who have your freedom to go and come as you please, but not so to me who can see it only through those window bars. Everywhere I go those hateful bars are before my mind, if not my eyes."

R.—She will be allowed to visit her sister will she?

J.B.—We hope so. Dr. Patterson

HAS SIGNED A CERTIFICATE

Mrs. Abraham Lincoln. Courtesy Library of Congress.

of her fitness to go; but she has not got it, and I have not, but he told me he had signed it. Mrs. Edwards wrote to her that she could come and live with her, and it is expected that when Robert Lincoln returns from the East, about the middle of this week, he will go to Batavia and accompany his mother to Springfield.[m] But I shall not feel safe when she is out.

DR. PATTERSON IS A VERY PECULIAR MAN.

I know that some letters she has sent have not been allowed to reach her friends, and some that have been sent her have not reached her. You can't tell what motives may tend to keep her there. Human nature is human nature. But if she is not soon out, there will be startling developments not to be mentioned now. Let her get out of danger first.[13]

In this way the storm gathered. Naturally, the press took sides. Some agreed with Dr. Patterson and Robert Lincoln. Others championed the cause of the martyred President's widow. Some newspapers called my grandparents "meddling old busy bodies," and "rand sentimentalists," and worse. Others assailed Robert Lincoln.[n]

That it was a storm cannot be denied, and there were tempestuous elements on both sides. To keep the record clear, to be just to all concerned, I would like to set forth the correspondence between Robert Todd Lincoln and Dr. Patterson with my grandparents without comment.

No one of them seems to have hesitated in preserving his thoughts upon paper, and any comment of mine would be anticlimactic.

m. Robert was with his family on vacation at Rye Beach, New Hampshire. When he left Chicago in mid-August, Dr. Patterson was of the opinion that Mary should stay at Bellevue Place, while Elizabeth Edwards had refused a visit from her sister. While Robert was away, his aunt told him she changed her mind and Mary could now come to visit (but not permanently live), and Patterson—frazzled by all the publicity—said Mary was stable enough to give the visit a try. When Robert returned to Chicago on Sept. 1, he was shocked and annoyed by what he termed "the extraordinary performances of the Bradwells."[12]

n. The *Chicago Tribune* called the Bradwells "intermeddling mischief-makers" and "intermeddling scandalizers"; the *Illinois State Journal* called them "busybodies"; and the *Boston Globe* called the Bradwells' statements and accusations "an outrage" and "utterly untrue." No newspaper stories "assailing" Robert Lincoln's conduct could be located other than the *Chicago Times*'s general suggestion (without naming Robert Lincoln) that Mary should be released. Elizabeth Edwards's two daughters visited Mary on Aug. 19 and told the physician that the widow's relatives "are satisfied with what has been done in Mrs. Lincoln's case, and would feel obliged to Mrs. B if she would mind her own business and not meddle with Mrs. L. They say also that Mrs. B. wrote a very mean letter to Mrs. Edwards, and I understood them to intimate that she charged unkind or improper treatment toward Mrs. L. while here."[14]

6

In 1875 the position of Abraham Lincoln in American history still was highly controversial. People gifted with far vision regarded him much as we of today regard him, but there were thousands, yes hundreds of thousands, who continued to speak of him as a tyrant, a butcher, a spoilsman.[1]

Abraham Lincoln was dead and the grave protected him, but Mary Todd Lincoln, his widow, lived—if incarceration in a retreat for the insane can be called living—and suffered for him.

There were friends who loved her, who believed her to be the victim of a monstrous miscarriage of justice, and they were striving for her release.

It was inevitable that there would be opposition, strong opposition, and the letters I set forth here are ample proof of the strife. I have promised to refrain from comment, and I shall after I call attention to the dates of the letters, their authors, their contents, and certain facts involving my possession of them. I do feel that my holding of Robert Todd Lincoln's letters to his mother should be explained.

Mary Lincoln sent them to my grandfather—who, you will recall, was her legal adviser at the time—to be used as evidence to procure her release. The letters follow.

Batavia, Ill.
Aug. 13, 1875.
Mrs. Myra Bradwell,

Madam:

Dr. Patterson encloses to me your note asking for Mrs. Edwards's letter.[a] He had already some days past sent the letter to me to be

6

a. Elizabeth Edwards's letter to Myra Bradwell, Aug. 3, 1875 (see chapter 3), in which she voiced her disagreement over Mary Lincoln's commitment. Myra Bradwell showed the letter to Dr. Patterson as "proof" that Mary's family did not think her situation was proper; Bradwell told him to send it to Robert Lincoln and, evidently, then return it to her. Robert wrote to his aunt Elizabeth on Aug. 7 in response to seeing her letter to Myra Bradwell. His letter was one of the longest, most revealing letters of the entire episode, and explained his actions. "There is no need of my rehearsing ten years of our domestic history. If it has caused you one tenth of the grief it has caused me, you will remember it," Robert wrote. He considered it a "blessing" to put his mother at Bellevue, the facility and superintendent of which he described at length. Robert also criticized the interference of Myra Bradwell, saying he felt the quiet and absence of any chance of excitement at the sanitarium had improved his mother's condition. Dr. Patterson, however, was afraid that the Bradwells' visits and manner would undo any progress made. "What trouble Mrs. Bradwell may give me with her interference I cannot foretell," Robert wrote. "I understand she is a high priestess in a gang of Spiritualists and from what I have heard it is to their interest that my mother should be at liberty to control herself and her property." This was, of course, one of the reasons Robert had his mother committed in the first place. His mother's "feebleness of mind," as Robert called it, and her belief in Spiritualism made her susceptible to thieves and sharpers. But he also feared for his mother's safety, saying that if she were freed she would immediately go to Europe, "and such a thing in her present state of mind would be productive of the most disturbing events to us all." Robert reiterated that he had no objection to Mary's visit to Springfield—in fact he thought it would be beneficial—and he invited his aunt to visit Bellevue Place and see the sanitarium for herself, rather than rely on the words of Myra Bradwell.[2]

transmitted to you, and the delay is caused by my accidental neglect or forgetfulness for which I beg to be excused.

Very respectfully yours,
Robert T. Lincoln.[3]

The day after the foregoing note was penned, Robert Todd Lincoln again writes my grandmother, and this seems to be the beginning of the break between him and Dr. Patterson and my grandparents. In this letter also he speaks of a Mrs. Edwards letter but whether or not it is the one referred to in earlier correspondence I cannot say.

That Robert Lincoln did not approve of the efforts of Judge Bradwell and his wife to free Mrs. Lincoln is evident in every line of his letter.

Chicago, Aug. 14th 1875.
Mrs. Myra Bradwell,

Madam:

Your note came here in my absence. On yesterday I received a letter from my Aunt Mrs. Edwards, which I gave this morning to Dr. Patterson.[b] I regret beyond measure that my Aunt is not able to aid me, as she says that her health is such that she cannot assume the responsibility. I had hoped for a possibility of benefit from my mother's apparent desire to renew her proper relations with her sister. I hope my Aunt may be able to come up here soon as I have invited her to do.

I visited my mother on yesterday and I could not help observing with pain, a renewal in a degree of the same appearances which marked her in May and which I had not noticed in my last few visits. I do not know of any outside reason for this unless it is the constant excitement she has been in since your first visit. I am persuaded that you wish only her good and that you recognize the responsibility which is on me and which I cannot shift or divide.[c]

When you asked me a few days ago[c] whether I objected to your visiting her I said I only desired that you would be prudent in your conversation with her and would not carry letters for her. In

b. The letter said, "My dear Robert, I received this morning, for the first time, a letter from your mother, and writes lovingly, and very urgently upon the subject of her release. I wish she could be persuaded to be calm, and contented for a while longer—if she complained of physical suffering, her detention could be put upon that ground, but she assures me, that her health is perfect, and her mind entirely sane. The enclosed note, to be handed to Mrs. Bradwell, if here, or otherwise mailed to Chicago. As I do not fully understand the rules of the institution at Batavia, I have concluded to send it to you to deliver, if you see proper. I would prefer that your mother should not see my letters to you wherein I so fully express myself about her mental condition, both now, and in the past. I am unwilling to excite her by intimating anything unpleasant, when she seems disposed to be amiable."[4]

c. This statement is indicative of Robert's Victorian sense of duty regarding his mother's situation. He believed it was his duty—and no one else's—to care for and protect her, and he made other statements to this same effect multiple times. On June 1 he told his mother's friend Sally Orne, "The responsibility that has been and is now on me is one that I would gladly share if it was possible to do so, but being alone as I am, I can only do my duty as it is given me to see it, trusting that I am guided for the best." On August 7 he wrote his aunt Elizabeth Edwards, "Rightly or wrongly I consider that I alone must assume the entire and absolute charge of her unfortunate situation and I must deal with it as my condition allows me to do. I am alone held responsible and I cannot help it. . . . I have done my duty as I best know and Providence must take care of the rest." In November he wrote his uncle Ninian Edwards, "There is no person upon whom lies the responsibility and duty of protecting her when she needs it, except myself."[5]

d. During Robert and Myra's August 10 meeting. See annotation p on page 71.

view of what I have seen and which I regard as a partial destruction of the good accomplished by two months and a half of quiet and freedom from all chance of excitement, I am compelled to request that you visit her less often and not at all with persons with whom I am not acquainted and especially that you do not aid her in corresponding with persons other than her relations. As to them Dr. Patterson will mail unopened as many letters as she desires to write.

Very respectfully yours,
Robert T. Lincoln.[e]

On August 15, Robert Lincoln wrote to his mother at Batavia. His letter informs her that the visit to Springfield she had set her heart upon was not to be made, and he chides her for her reluctance to remain at the insane asylum.

Chicago, Aug. 15th, 1875.

My dear Mother:

Dr. Patterson gave me your note yesterday. I am dreadfully disappointed that Aunt Lizzie (Mrs. Edwards) writes me that she is not well enough to have you visit her just now,[f] but I am going to try to arrange it with her for very soon. There is nothing I want so much as to have you with her for I am sure nothing would do you more good.

Mamie (Robert T. Lincoln's daughter, Mary) has put something in an envelope which she calls a letter to you and says I must send it—so here it is. I have not seen it but I doubt if you can read it.

You must trust me that I can and will do everything that is for your good and you must not allow yourself to think otherwise, for in that way you will only retard the recovery I am looking for. Your stay with Dr. Patterson has plainly benefited you and you must not undo all that has been done.

Affectionately Yours
R. T. L.[8]

e. Robert's restrictions on the Bradwells were not only because of their general agitating influence on Mary Lincoln but also because Mrs. Bradwell brought the *Chicago Times* reporter to Bellevue Place on Aug. 7.[6]

f. Elizabeth wrote to Robert, "When your poor mother proposed a visit to me, I felt that I must respond in a kind manner; supposing that if the visit, was permitted, she would be in charge of a responsible person, and taken back again, for a continuation of treatment. . . . I am unwilling to urge any steps, or assume any responsibility, in her case. My present feeble health, causing such nervous prostration, as would render me, a most unfit person, to control an unsound mind. I am now satisfied, that understanding her propensities, as you do, the course you have decided upon, is the surest and wisest."[7]

During this period both my grandparents were urging Dr. Patterson and Mr. Lincoln to allow Mary Lincoln to leave the institution.[g] In a final effort to prevent this, Dr. Patterson wrote my grandfather, practically demanding that the latter take no further part in the controversy. His letter, which was widely quoted in the press at the time, follows:

Batavia, Ill.,
Aug. 18, 1875.
Hon. J. B. Bradwell,

My dear Sir:

In regard to the case of Mrs. Lincoln allow me to say that I see no good to her but harm only in discussing *with her* the question of her removal from this place. It tends to keep her mind in a constant ferment over questions which should not be determined by an insane mind, questions which should never have been discussed with her. Promises should never have been made to her, the fulfillment of which could by possible circumstances pass beyond the control of those who made them.

I am quite willing to believe that the object of your visits and the numerous letters of Mrs. Bradwell are well meant and not designed to promote unrest and discontent. But I have become fully convinced that such is their tendency and result. My opinion is that for the present at least these visits should be discontinued. Mrs. Lincoln may be written to assigning reasons for not repeating visits.

I understand that R. T. Lincoln, Conservator of Mrs. Lincoln, will be absent from home about two weeks. I will suggest that, at least, until his return, Mrs. Lincoln should be simply let alone.

I have written the above in no unkind spirit, but from a sense of duty only to my patient.

Mrs. Lincoln has repeatedly said to me that you have in your possession an important paper that belongs to her. She again alluded to it today, saying "Judge Bradwell has again forgotten to bring my paper."[h] If you have any paper that belongs to her, *that*

g. Their efforts included newspaper articles and interviews, and a flurry of letters and visits to all the principal people involved: Robert Lincoln, Mary Lincoln, Dr. Patterson, and Elizabeth Edwards.

h. Mary's will, which he helped her write in 1872–73 and had in his possession.

Dr. Richard J. Patterson, proprietor of Bellevue Place sanitarium in Batavia, Illinois, and one of the most respected mental health experts of the Midwest in his day. Patterson was Mary's doctor during her four-month stay in the asylum.
Courtesy Batavia Historical Society

she ought to have, perhaps it may be well to send it to her or to me and thus relieve her seeming anxiety.

Very Respectfully,
R. J. Patterson.[9]

The next day my grandfather replied and threatened a habeas corpus if Mrs. Lincoln were not liberated and allowed to visit her sister.

Aug. 19th, 1875
Dr. R. J. Patterson.

My dear sir:

I have rec'd your letter stating that you can see no good to Mrs. Lincoln but harm only in discussing with her the question of her removal from your place and that promises should never have been made to her the fulfillment of which could by possible circumstances pass beyond the control of those who made them, etc. etc.

Now, Sir, who was it but yourself that told Mrs. Lincoln and also myself that she was in a condition to visit her sister Mrs. Edwards at Springfield and that you had written a letter to her son Robert to that effect and Mrs. Bradwell to carry out the expressed wish of Mrs. Lincoln went to Springfield to see Mrs. Edwards to see if she would take her sister.

I was assured by her that she would do so if brought by her son and so wrote him day before yesterday. Now Dr. if you have the good of Mrs. Lincoln at heart I am sure you will see that she is taken to her sister's. It is in accordance with your letter. I am satisfied that Mrs. Lincoln does not require to be confined in a house for the insane and that it would be greatly for her good to be allowed to visit her relatives and friends and she pines for liberty.

Some of the best medical men in America say that it is shameful to lock Mrs. Lincoln up behind grates as she has been and I concur with them. I believe that such confinement is injurious to her in the extreme and calculated to drive her insane. Are you not going

The home of Ninian and Elizabeth Edwards in Springfield, Illinois. It was here that Abraham Lincoln and Mary Todd originally met in 1839 and married in 1842. It also was here in 1875 where Mary Lincoln and James and Myra Bradwell tried to get the former First Lady relocated after an early release from Bellevue Place sanitarium. In this they succeeded, and Mary lived with her sister and brother-in-law from September 1875 through September 1876, when she left for Europe. Photo courtesy Abraham Lincoln Presidential Library.

to allow her to visit her relatives to see if it will not benefit her or will you take the responsibility and run the risk of the American people saying hereafter that it was the restraint of your institution that injured Mrs. Lincoln and proved her ruin.

Should you not allow her to visit Mrs. Edwards and insist on keeping her in close confinement and I should be satisfied that the good of Mrs. Lincoln required it as I certainly shall unless there is a change in her condition. I as her legal adviser will see if a habeas corpus cannot open the doors of Mrs. Lincoln's prison home.

I am etc. etc.

James B. Bradwell.[10]

This exchange was picked up by the newspapers and served to reopen the entire Mary Lincoln controversy. Some papers that had defended Robert Lincoln at the insanity trial were now sympathetic to Mrs. Lincoln, but there were many who still supported her son.

It did result, however, in releasing Mary Lincoln, although, of course, she continued to be regarded as officially insane.[i]

I am unable to give the exact date she left Dr. Patterson's sanitarium but Mrs. Eleanor Gridley, author of *From Log Cabin To White House* has informed me that it was early in September 1875.[j]

Mrs. Gridley, a close friend of my grandparents, says that Mrs. Lincoln went directly to my grandmother's home and remained there some time before joining her sister, Mrs. Edwards, in Springfield.[k] There is no record of a habeas corpus having been procured, and it would seem that the weight of public opinion caused Robert Lincoln to consent to his mother's liberation before her friends resorted to legal procedure.

i. Untrue. Judge Bradwell's threat did not initiate Mary's release. In fact, Dr. Patterson wrote a public response to Bradwell's threat in which he dared him to try it, which Bradwell did not.[11] It was because of the Bradwells' interference, however, that Mary Lincoln was released from the sanitarium eight months early. Robert simply realized that there was no return to a simple, quiet stay at Bellevue Place for his mother. As Patterson told Robert, Mary was now constantly agitated by the promise of Springfield and would only continue to be agitated, even if all communication with the Bradwells were stopped. In such a state of constant ferment, her health would fail to improve, and perhaps would decline. The situation also had altered in that Elizabeth Edwards now said Mary could come and visit; even Dr. Patterson changed his mind. He told Robert, "Now that so much is said about Mrs. Lincoln's removal to Springfield, I think it would be well if she could go at once." Robert then consulted other mental health experts about the safety of allowing his mother to leave the sanitarium, to which the response was she should not go. Robert decided to send her anyway. However, her time at Springfield was arranged and understood by all to be a visit, not a relocation.[12]

j. Sept. 10, 1875.

k. Mary Lincoln left Bellevue Place Sanitarium a little less than four months after her trial and commitment, with three trunks of possessions and two female attendants. She met Robert at the Chicago train station, spent the night, and arrived in Springfield on the morning of Sept. 11. While it is possible that Robert allowed his mother to spend her first night out of the sanitarium at the Bradwell home on Michigan Avenue, considering all the trouble the couple caused, it is highly unlikely that Robert would have taken his mother there.[13]

7

Continued protestations and demands for action on the part of my grandparents at last had released Mary Todd Lincoln from Dr. Patterson's private sanitarium for the insane at Batavia, Ill., after four months incarceration there.

What joy to her to be once more free, to view the sunlight through windows without bars! But there were limits to her freedom for, although she could visit her friends and relatives at her pleasure, she was not mistress of her business affairs.

The state still held her to be insane and subject to the directions and orders of her son, Robert Todd Lincoln, who had been named her conservator.[a] She could conduct no business because, in the eyes of the law, she was incompetent to manage her estate.

This situation was to bring about a very awkward state of affairs between Mrs. Lincoln and Judge Bradwell, my grandfather, who had championed her cause from the first.

After a short visit with my grandparents, she went to the home of her sister in Springfield, Ill., from where she carried on her correspondence with them.[b] Her first letter from there after her release follows.

November 11, 1875.
Judge Bradwell,

My dear Friend:

A long and weary time has passed since I last saw you. Knowing well the interest you have taken in my sad fate, I feel assured that

7

a. Robert had posted a $150,000 bond as conservator, backed financially by two suretors. Under Illinois state law, Robert's conservatorship would last for a minimum of one year, during which time he had sole power to collect income, pay bills, and otherwise manage his mother's estate.[1]

b. Pritchard does not state here that the Bradwells had not written or visited Mary once in the two months between her release from Bellevue Place and the date of her letter, nor would they resume communication until June 1876. Given the Bradwells' zealous efforts to advocate Mary's sanity and release from Bellevue, why would they have abandoned her? Evidence suggests they may have been abiding by an agreement with Robert Lincoln to stop communicating with Mary. Critical newspapers, however, had accused the Bradwells of being attention-seeking meddlers who would lose interest in Mary Lincoln and her situation once the sensation had ended.

you will be pleased to hear that I am in perfect health. I am staying with my sister, Mrs. Edwards, who has always been tenderly attached to me.

I am now writing at the suggestion of Mrs. N. W. Edwards, who is desirous that you should send me that *will* you wrote for me many months since.[c] You will remember that I left it in your charge. Please send it by return of mail.

What can I say to your dear wife? The sorrow which has been mine for the last six months has been in a measure alleviated by the friendship of such noble hearts as yours. I feel assured you will reply to this note at once without even mentioning that you have heard from me.

The paths of life have become very rough to me since the most loving and devoted husband and children have been called from my side. In the great hereafter when I am reunited to my beloved ones, we will then know why the gracious Father has caused such deep affliction. Be kind enough to enclose the will to Mr. N. W. Edwards.

Yours very truly,
Mary Lincoln[4]

Write me quietly, both of you.

On December 1, she wrote a somewhat perempt[ory] note to my grandfather which read:

Judge Bradwell:

A month since I wrote you requesting you to send me the *will* which you wrote and which I entrusted to your care.

Please send it to me at once and greatly oblige,

Your friend,
Mrs. A. Lincoln[d]

I know the will to which she refers was in my grandfather's possession because it is now in mine. My mother gave it to me with the Mary Lincoln letters and, with it, an explanation of its presence among her papers.

c. Mary apparently wanted her will at this time so she could rewrite it and disinherit her traitorous son. By this time, after two months at the Edwards house, Mary Lincoln had, according to her sister, returned to her more rational, personable, and even cheerful self of past years. Just one week prior to this letter, Elizabeth Edwards told her nephew, "I have no hesitation, in pronouncing her sane, and far more reasonable, and gentle, than in former years." The sole subject—according to the Edwardses—which upset Mary Lincoln was her finances. Under the Illinois insanity statute, she had no right to control her own money and property. That power was exclusive to her court-appointed conservator, her son Robert, and such a situation, according to Elizabeth Edwards, was "to [Mary's] proud spirit . . . very galling."[2] Mary Lincoln believed that Robert had had her committed so he could steal her money, and Elizabeth appears to have suggested revising the will as a way to mollify her anger. Robert himself, seeing his mother's irrational—to his mind—anger and paranoia about her finances, suggested to the Edwardses that he be removed from his mother's will if it would satisfy her.[3]

d. Mary's note was terse because Bradwell had ignored her previous letter. He did finally send her the document in mid-December.[5] As the will shows, she did not disinherit Robert, and it appears that she did not change the will at all. At some point, although it is unclear when or how, Mary Lincoln returned her will to Judge Bradwell, and he kept it in his possession. Evidence suggests, however, that Bradwell was not supposed to keep the will but put it in a safe-deposit box in the Fidelity Bank. When Mary first wrote her will in 1873, she also wrote a letter to be delivered to the Cook County judge upon her death, to inform him of her will and its location. The letter was delivered properly four days after Mary's death in 1882, but when Robert Lincoln went to the bank box, the will was not there.[6]

It was not forwarded to Mrs. Lincoln because Judge Bradwell had no legal right to do so. Mary Todd Lincoln, so far as the courts and the world at large were concerned, was an insane person, and it would have been highly unethical for grandfather to have sent her the document under such conditions.

There is no record of her ever again request[ing] it, and from her letter of November 11, it is evident that the desire to have it in her possession was not entirely her own.

The will never was probated. Two months after Mary Lincoln's death in Springfield, Robert Todd Lincoln petitioned the Sangamon County Court for and was granted letters of administration for his mother's estate.[7]

Upon being informed of this and realizing that Mrs. Lincoln's estate was now in the hands of her son, to whom she had originally willed it, my grandfather never brought out the will.

Because of his efforts on behalf of President Lincoln's widow, Judge Bradwell and his wife had been interviewed, criticized, yes, at times, almost hounded, and he saw no reason why he should needlessly subject his family to further unpleasant publicity.

Had he submitted the will for probate, it would have brought on another clash with Robert Lincoln, already in possession of the estate as administrator, and reopened the old, unpleasant controversy.

The story of Mary Lincoln, her insanity trial, her incarceration, all the old rancors and heartaches would have been bared to public view again, and he was convinced that silence was the better way.

I honor him for it.

Mary Lincoln's will, already fold-worn and time-stained, is undying evidence of the love she once bore her son, Robert Lincoln. It was executed July 23, 1873, is signed by Mary Lincoln, and is witnessed by my grandfather and grandmother.

It reads:

In the name of God, amen, I, Mary Lincoln, of the City of Chicago, County of Cook and State of Illinois, widow of the good and lamented Abraham Lincoln, the martyred President of the United States, realizing the uncertainty of life and the certainty of death, being of sound mind and memory and having fifty-six thousand

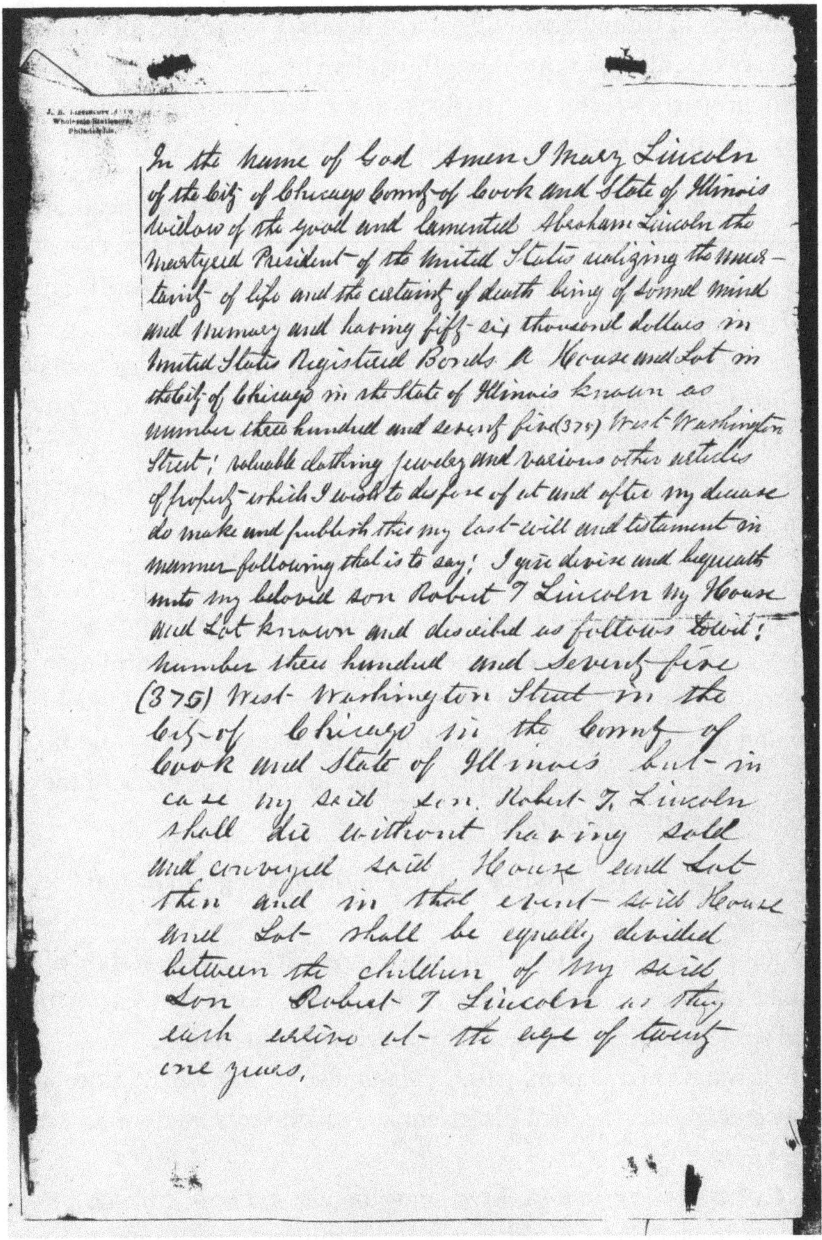

In the name of God Amen I Mary Lincoln of the City of Chicago County of Cook and State of Illinois widow of the good and lamented Abraham Lincoln the martyred President of the United States realizing the uncertainty of life and the certainty of death being of sound mind and memory and having fifty six thousand dollars in United States Registered Bonds A House and Lot in the City of Chicago in the State of Illinois known as number three hundred and seventy five (375) West Washington Street; valuable clothing jewelry and various other articles of property which I wish to dispose of at and after my decease do make and publish this my last will and testament in manner following that is to say: I give devise and bequeath unto my beloved son Robert T Lincoln my House and Lot known and described as follows to wit: number three hundred and Seventy five (375) West Washington Street in the City of Chicago in the County of Cook and State of Illinois but in case my said son Robert T. Lincoln shall die without having sold and conveyed said House and Lot then and in that event said House and Lot shall be equally divided between the children of my said Son Robert T Lincoln as they each arrive at the age of twenty one years.

First page of Mary Lincoln's will, which she wrote with the assistance of her legal advisor James Bradwell between 1872 and 1873. As Pritchard states, the will was not brought out at Mary's death in 1882, and in fact had never been seen by anyone outside the Bradwell family until the discovery of the Lincoln-Bradwell documents in 2005. Photo courtesy Library of Congress.

> dollars in United States Registered Bonds, a house and lot in the City of Chicago; valuable clothing, jewelry and various articles of property which I wish to dispose of at and after my decease do make and publish this my last will and testament.[8]

The Chicago house at No. 375 West Washington Street she bequeathed to Robert Lincoln; her remaining estate she left to Judge David Davis of the United States Supreme Court and her cousin Major John. T. Stuart as trustees to be distributed among Robert Lincoln's children.[e]

There is a codicil dated January 3, 1874, wherein Mrs. Lincoln makes a special bequest of a one-thousand-dollar United States Government bond to her infant grandson, [Abraham Lincoln II,] to be paid him upon his twenty-first birthday. She also directs that the interest be paid him semiannually for pocket money.

The flowing interesting passage also occurs in the codicil:

> Hereto attached is a paper of even date signed by my son's wife, Mary H. Lincoln, in which she says the names of my grandchildren for all time to come are Mary Lincoln and [Abraham] Lincoln and that their given names shall never be changed and no middle names ever added. It is my desire that no change be made in the names of my grandchildren.[f]

These are the outstanding features in the missing will of Mary Todd Lincoln.

Robert Lincoln's letters of administration put him in possession of the estate, his mother's chief interest at the time the document was written, and subsequent events show that it remained in his hands.

He was named as administrator September 28, 1882, and on November 6, two years later, he filed his inventory, which accounted for an estate of $84,035.[10]

He listed the estate in three items: bonds, $72,000; currency, $555; and personal effects, $5,000. Under the heading "Real Estate" there is, in Robert Lincoln's own handwriting, the entry, "none." The Chicago house [at 375 West Washington St] had been deeded to him several years before her death.[g]

e. Robert and Mary Harlan Lincoln had three children, although only two, Mary (born 1869) and Abraham II (born 1873), were alive at the time Mary Lincoln drew her will. The Lincolns' third child, Jessie, was born in 1875. Little is known about Mary Lincoln's relationship with her grandchildren. During her years in Europe she sent numerous items of clothing and gifts to Mamie, and some to Jack; but Mamie was the only one of Robert's children to truly know and remember her grandmother Lincoln. She visited with her before, during, and after her time in the sanitarium, but Mamie's memories may not have been that pleasant. Her cousin later recalled a conversation with Mamie concerning both sets of her grandparents, and while the youngest Mary told of how she loved the Harlans and admired Abraham Lincoln, "she did not speak of her Grandmother Lincoln," her cousin wrote. "I wonder now what the child's idea was of that inexplicable Mary Todd."[9]

f. Pritchard's manuscript mistakenly says the grandson's name was "Robert Lincoln" rather than "Abraham."

g. Mary actually sold the house to Robert in April 1874 for $10,000. Robert paid no money up front but paid a monthly mortgage to Mary (which she called "rent") beginning April 27, 1874, to be completed by May 1, 1881. His payments, which did not include interest, began at $125 per month but were increased to $150 at Mary's request. Robert rented out the house to various tenants until he eventually sold it.[11]

I have considered it proper to present Mary Lincoln's lost will here, in conjunction with her letters to my grandfather requesting it. Now I shall return to the last letter I quoted, that curt little note of December 1, 1875, signed so stiltedly, "Mrs. A. Lincoln."

She was, you will recall, still officially insane, but her friends—they were a growing number now—were constantly striving to alter that status. Mary Lincoln herself was anxious to regain control of her affairs and was particularly worried because valuable keepsakes and documents, most of them mementoes of her illustrious husband's official life, were being kept from her.[h]

Repeatedly she requested her son to send these to her, and the records of the Cook County Court show that he twice received permission of this tribunal to give them into her hands. On December 10, 1875, Robert Lincoln as conservator was granted permission to send his mother nine trunks containing personal effects which were stored under his name in a Chicago storehouse. Again on December 15, the same year, he was authorized to give her a tin box containing jewelry and personal effects, also stored in his care.[i] Mrs. Lincoln's later letters to my grandparents, which I shall include in this series, contain pointed comment on these personal treasures.

The Cook County Court records show no development in the case of Mary Lincoln from that December 15th petition of her conservator son until June 15, 1876, nor have I any correspondence to bridge that gap of time.[j]

On June 15 Mary Todd Lincoln was declared sane! Her estate was returned to her own keeping, and she could take up again freedom in its fullness.[k]

The record discloses that Ninian W. Edwards, her brother-in-law, was one of the principal witnesses in her behalf. It is his affidavit I give here:

> Mrs. Lincoln has been with me for nine or ten months, and her friends all think she is a proper person to take charge of her own affairs. She has been with me about nine months, and her friends, all of them, recognize that she is a fit person to take care of and manage her own affairs. That she is now in such condition that

h. Untrue. Robert sent her all she asked for, and then some. He refused to send her items she claimed were hers or that Robert and his wife had "stolen" from her, when in fact they had been gifts she gave them. "Your mother for the last two or three weeks has been very much embittered against you," Ninian Edwards wrote Robert in Dec. 1875, "and the more you have yielded the more immeasurable she seems to be." On Feb. 7, 1876, Robert sent his mother so many boxes of her demanded possessions—paintings, household items, and books—that Elizabeth Edwards complained of the clutter in her house. Robert apologized, but was undeterred in his course of accommodating his mother, even though her demands offended and hurt him. "Although I considered these things as much my own as though I had bought them, I gave them to her desiring to gratify her as far as I can," Robert explained. But as soon as he sent her the boxes, she immediately sent another letter, more than a dozen pages long, filled with more demands. "Everything that we can recognize was a present at one time or another, many things neither my wife nor I remember ever seeing, many other (dress goods & the like) are worn out & forgotten. Apart from these considerations the whole demand is so unreasonable in the light of any service that the things could be to her or that she could properly make of them in her situation that it is plainly irrational and the emanation of an insane mind."[12]

i. Pritchard here omits the fact that Robert *informed* the court of his mother's letters as soon as he received them and *requested* that he be *allowed* to send the possessions to her. He was not ordered by the court to do so, as Pritchard suggests.[13]

j. Much happened between Mary and Robert from January to June 1876, with a large amount of correspondence to explain it, although none of it involved Myra or James Bradwell. Mary grew increasingly hostile toward her son, and her growing antipathy was paralleled by a dramatic increase in her shopping. She spent at least half of every day with dressmakers and in stores, hid the actual extent of her purchasing from her sister and brother-in-law, and instructed the merchants to do the same. "I am sorry to say that your mother has for the last month been very much embittered against you, and has on several occasions said that she has hired two men to take your life," Ninian Edwards wrote Robert in mid-January. "On this morning we learned that she carries a pistol in her pocket. . . . She says she will never again allow you to come into her presence. We do not know what is best to be done." Robert's reaction to the threat was surprisingly altruistic. "Your letters . . . give me great concern, not for myself but I fear that something unforeseen may happen," he wrote. Robert added, as a subtle jab at the Edwardses for their meddling, "The doctors whom we consulted last spring were very urgent in expressing their opinion that no one could foretell the possible freaks which might take possession of my mother and that she should be placed

> she can manage her own affairs. She has not spent all that she was allowed to spend during the last year and we all think she is in condition to take care of her own affairs.[16]

What other testimony may have been brought out does not appear in the record, but I quote the docket entry in full.

> A petition having been filed in this court on this day by Mary Lincoln who was heretofore upon trial by a jury found to be insane and incapable of managing and controlling her estate, alleging that she is now a proper person to have the care and management of her estate and praying that Robert T. Lincoln, who was heretofore appointed by this court as her conservator, may be removed from his said office.
>
> Now comes the said Robert T. Lincoln conservator aforesaid and waives service of notice and enters his appearance. And the said Mary Lincoln, petitioner, comes by Leonard Swett, esquire, her attorney. Whereupon it is ordered by the court that a jury be called to try said cause in pursuance of the statute in such case made and provided.
>
> And thereupon come the jurors of a jury of good and lawful men to wit; R. H. Paddock, a doctor of medicine; D. J. Weatherhead, S. F. Knowles, Cyrus Gleason, W. R. Heron, D. Kimball, R. F. Wild, William G. Lyon, C. H. Chapin, H. Dahl, W. S. Dunham and William W. Roberts, who after being duly empanelled, tried and sworn according to law, and having heard the evidence adduced and the arguments of counsel retire in charge of an officer of the court to consider their verdict, and thereupon return into court and render their verdict in form and words as follows to wit:
>
> We the undersigned jurors in the case wherein Mary Lincoln who was heretofore found to be insane and who is now alleged to be restored to reason having heard the evidence in said cause find that the said Mary Lincoln is restored to reason and is capable to manage and control her estate.
>
> Which verdict is signed by each of the jurors aforesaid.

where no catastrophe could happen." The main part of Mary's anger was over Robert's control of her estate. By law, he could not be removed as her conservator until June; he offered to resign and let one of Mary's defenders take his place—namely, Jacob Bunn or John M. Palmer—but nobody would accept the responsibility.[14]

k. The trial was a simple affair that consisted of Mary's submitted petition asking for the discharge of her conservator, the testimony of Ninian Edwards as to Mary's fitness for the discharge, the consent of Robert for his removal as conservator, and his accounting of her estate. Newspapers reported that the trial took less time than the actual empanelling of the jury.[15]

> And thereupon it is considered by the court upon the verdict aforesaid that the said Mary Lincoln is restored to reason and is now capable of managing and controlling her estate.[l]
>
> And thereupon said conservator presents to the court his final account showing receipts amounting to $11,140.35 and disbursements amounting to $11,140.35 of which amount the sum of $4,264.38 was expended for an investment in United States Bonds.
>
> And it appearing to the court from an examination of said account that the same is full, just and true, it is ordered that said account be approved, recorded and placed on file. And it is further ordered that said conservator be discharged from his said office upon filing herein the receipt of said Mary Lincoln for all money and property in his hands belonging to her estate.[18]

Robert Lincoln's receipt from his mother covers but two items, $61,500 worth of United States bonds and his own obligation on which there remained unpaid $7,250.[m]

His inventory discloses one most interesting fact in connection with Mary Todd Lincoln's trial for insanity.

In an earlier installment I described the action to declare her insane and reprinted much of the evidence submitted. It will be remembered that Samuel M. Turner, manager of the Grand Pacific Hotel in Chicago, where Mrs. Lincoln was living May 19, 1875, the date of her trial, and three other hotel employees all testified that she had complained of being followed by a man and this repeated complaint of surveillance was looked upon as one proof of her mental derangement.

But there seems to be conclusive evidence in Robert Todd Lincoln's inventory that his mother was followed, for, in his final accounting, he lists a payment of $151 to "A. Pinkerton" for the services and expenses and of a special attendant *covering the precise period that Mrs. Lincoln complained of being followed!*[n]

l. The court was not, in fact, empanelled to decide on Mary's sanity or insanity, but only to decide whether or not she was fit to control her own property and therefore to have her conservator discharged. Robert's notice of waiver was labeled "In the matter of Mary Lincoln to be declared to be a proper person to have the charge of her property." Then why did the jury declare her "restored to reason"? Unfortunately, the county court records offer no explanation. However, the Illinois lunacy statute stated that only a person who was declared restored to reason could have his property restored to him. The Illinois Supreme Court had ruled in 1872 that the statute voided all contracts made by persons declared insane. These two points of law make clear that Mary's property could not be restored until she was declared sane. Therefore, a logical conclusion would be that the court clerk, who drew up the verdict and presumably understood the law, was the one who included the phrase "restored to reason." In fact, Ninian Edwards's affidavit, labeled "In the matter of the restoration to reason of Mary Lincoln," was handwritten by the court clerk. Interestingly, all parties involved in the trial were surprised by the jury's verdict. "They were not called upon to try the question of her sanity, and [I] regret very much that the verdict stated that she was 'restored to reason,'" Ninian Edwards wrote to Robert Lincoln two days after the hearing. Mary Lincoln was furious at the verdict because it implied that she had regained a sanity that she never conceded she had lost.[17]

m. Robert presented to the court his official accounting of his mother's estate, which totaled $81,390.35 in cash, stocks and bonds, and personal possessions—an increase of nearly $8,000 under his stewardship. This increase was due in part to Robert's investment in additional government bonds and in part to the accumulated interest on her total bonds. Robert also refused thousands of dollars in his entitled compensation as conservator.[19]

n. In May 1875, Robert hired the Pinkerton National Detective Agency whose "sole duty" was to have a man watch his mother as a sort of guardian "when she went out on the street." This fact was stated in open court during Mary's 1875 trial. What Pritchard leaves out is that Mary complained of being followed by various men—not one specific man—*before* Robert hired the Pinkertons; this is clear from the trial testimony. As soon as she arrived in Chicago in March 1875, Mary told Robert that a man had poisoned her coffee on the train ride north, and that a "wandering Jew" had taken her pocket book on the train but would return it later—both of these statements she repeated to other people. The Grand Pacific Hotel manager testified that Mary complained of strange men in the halls whom she feared would molest her, but when he searched the halls with Mrs. Lincoln there was no one there.[20]

8

Mary Todd Lincoln at liberty, possessing the signed verdict of a jury pronouncing her sane, and freed by court order from a conservatorship that had deprived her of any voice in her own affairs, became a different woman.

To her these meant vindication, justice, and she accepted them eagerly. Her demeanor underwent an immediate change. Old traits that had not manifested themselves in years became apparent in her actions and her correspondence. She was more nearly like the tempestuous, headstrong Mary Todd of the Kentucky days than at any time since the death of Lincoln.[a]

She believed she had been unjustly, cruelly dealt with, and this, no doubt, made doubly bitter the memory of older injustices and cruelties. She was resentful, sharply, scornfully resentful, and she did not hesitate to spread her feelings upon paper.

In view of the efforts my grandparents had made not only to liberate her from an insane asylum but to have her legally restored to reason, it is natural, I think, that she turned to them for full expression of her thoughts.[b]

Nor did she delay long. Three days after her second trial she wrote my grandmother. A bitter letter? A challenging one? Yes, but the seeds of this bitterness, the urge to challenge, were sown months before during her captivity in Batavia.

She made no veiled insinuations. When did Mary Todd Lincoln ever mince words? She wrote wrathfully, pointedly, and placed the blame for what she considered to be gross wrongs squarely upon the shoulders of one man—her own son, Robert Todd Lincoln. Nor did she hold Leonard Swett, a former legal colleague of her dead husband's, entirely blameless.

8

a. In fact, Mary's demeanor changed significantly as soon as she removed to the Edwards home in Springfield in Sept. 1875. "We take daily rides, and your mother enjoys, without a doubt, the change in her habits," Elizabeth Edwards reported in mid-September. "She has dined at Mrs. Smith's, taken tea at our sister Francis's, and received every visitor, with a manifestation of cheerfulness, and pleasure, as has surprised me. . . . Thus far, she has shown herself very clear-headed." These good tidings must have continued through October and into early November, as no letters from that period are known to exist. Robert was surprised by this; he actually had predicted that his mother would shut herself in her room and refuse all visitors and invitations. However, he also said Mary could do anything to achieve a goal once determined, and, in this case, her goal was to prove that her son was wrong about how she would behave in Springfield.[1]

b. As previously noted, the Bradwells did not communicate with Mary Lincoln for nine months, from Sept. 1875 to June 1876, possibly due to an agreement with Robert Lincoln to stay away. This theory is bolstered by the fact that *the day after* Mary Lincoln was declared sane in June 1876, Myra Bradwell immediately broke her nine-month silence and wrote her vindicated friend a letter. The letter has never been found, but Mary Lincoln thanked Myra Bradwell for her "most welcome letter" in her correspondence to Myra on June 18. The two women then kept in contact until at least July 1878 (the date of their last known letter), and probably until Mary's death in 1882. Bradwell also ran a notice of the 1876 hearing restoring Mary Lincoln's rights and property in the *Chicago Legal News*. The article was a reprint of a *Chicago Times* article, with one paragraph added to explain the legal process necessary to remove a conservator.[2]

The first letter in which she speaks openly of these things is dated June 18, 1876, at Springfield and reads:

My dear Mrs. Bradwell:

Your most welcome letter, was received last evening and I am quickly demonstrating the pleasure it afforded me, by replying at once.

God is just, *retribution* must follow those who act wickedly in *this* life. Sooner or later compensation surely awaits those, who suffer unjustly, if not here, in a brighter and happier world.

The most villainous plot has come to a close, but on Friday morning, when the young man, who perpetrated it came down to S. (Springfield) when I looked into his face (at a slight distance you may be sure) I saw the reluctance, with which he yielded up what he so ignominiously fought for—my poor pittance, as the world goes—so far as wealth is concerned "a widow's mite," my bonds.[c]

Prayers will scarcely avail in his case I think. My heart fails me, when I think of the contrast between himself and my noble glorious husband, and my precious sons, who have only "gone before," and are anxiously, I am sure, awaiting the reunion, where no more separation comes—and as I told him (R. T. L.) he could not approach us in the other world—on account of his heartless conduct, to the wife of a man who worshipped me—as well as my blessed sons did.

This one as my beloved husband always said, was so very different from the rest of us. Prided himself on his philosophical nature—not satisfied with the fortunes I bequeathed him *in one* morning,[d] desiring the rest, brought false charges against me. The only trouble about me, in all my sorrows and bereavements has been, that my mind has always been too *clear* and remembrances have always been too keen, in the midst of my griefs.

As to *Swett* he has proved himself to be, the most unmitigated scoundrel and *hell* will be his portion and doubtless he will have company. Never could such a creature approach my husband, who loved me so devotedly—in the other life.[e] I have my dear friend,

c. Robert went to Springfield on June 16, the morning after his mother's second trial, to personally return her bonds to her. Mary must have treated him harshly, for Ninian Edwards wrote to Robert the next day that he was "pained to hear of your mother's treatment of you."[3] In a separate letter on the same day, Edwards told Robert, "Your mother is in good humor again, and we are in hopes that she will in a very short time be reconciled to you."[4]

d. This probably refers to the division of Tad's estate after his death in July 1871. By state law, Mary was entitled to two-thirds of his $35,750 estate and Robert to one-third, but she chose to split the amount equally with her oldest son. Robert called this "very generous," as it "makes a difference of about $7,000."[5]

e. Leonard Swett was another in a long list of people whom Mary Lincoln declared she admired, loved, or was devoted to—as long as they could help her—but if and when they acted against her wishes on any subject for any reason, she turned against them viciously and permanently. Mary had in fact sought Swett's help in 1867 in her battle for a pension from the U.S. Congress, and told him more than once at that time that he was one of the friends "whom my dearly beloved husband, most loved."[6] Mary also mentioned Swett's close friendship with her husband—this time as an accusation of treachery—on May 19, 1875, when he came to her hotel room to bring her to the court for her insanity trial: "And you my husband's friend, you would take me and lock me up in an asylum, would you?" she screamed at him.[7]

a very great favor to ask of yourself, your good husband and the gentleman, who called with you at B (Batavia)—the City Editor, (The editor's name was Franc B. Wilkie) of the *Times*.

If I were to tell you *three all* the utterances of this man R. T. L. you would *not refrain* from writing the *latter* person up, *without* a day's delay. Your pen is sharp, so is Judge Bradwell's, so is the Editor's, just named, of course you would not wish your names to appear, but you will not fail me, I am sure, *now*, is the time, have justice rendered me, my dearly loved friends. See the City Editor of the Times, before the close *of the day*, when you receive *this* letter. I have been a deeply wronged woman, by one, for whom I would have poured out my life's blood.

R. T. L.'s *imprecations* against you all have been very great, only on account of your being my true friends. *Do not* allow a day to pass, before this writing *is done* and forwarded in *every direction*. Let not *his wickedness* triumph. It appears there is no law for the widow—in this land, and I solemnly pledge my word as an honorable woman, that *not one* word shall ever escape my lips—not a person in *this* house or elsewhere about any article or the probabl[e] author, that may be published.

My sister Mrs. E. sat by *me* on Friday, for about an hour and a half and in a quiet, composed and I trust lady like manner I gave expression to my feelings as to sins he had committed against a broken hearted woman who had been called upon to give up, all her dearly beloved ones, for *the time* being only—and I asked him to look upon my bleached hair—which he had entirely caused with the past sorrowful year.

Write, fail me not, I pray you, *any delay* would be grievous I assure you. So much I have to tell you. Kiss your sweet lovely daughter for me. Would to heaven I could see you. Best regards to your husband—*fail me* not. Always your most affectionate friend.

Mary Lincoln[8]

I enclose this article from yesterday's Forward. Phillips,[f] I believe, wrote it. Write stronger. I am sure you will. Burn this scrawl. You will, especially on the last page, be unable to decipher it I fear.

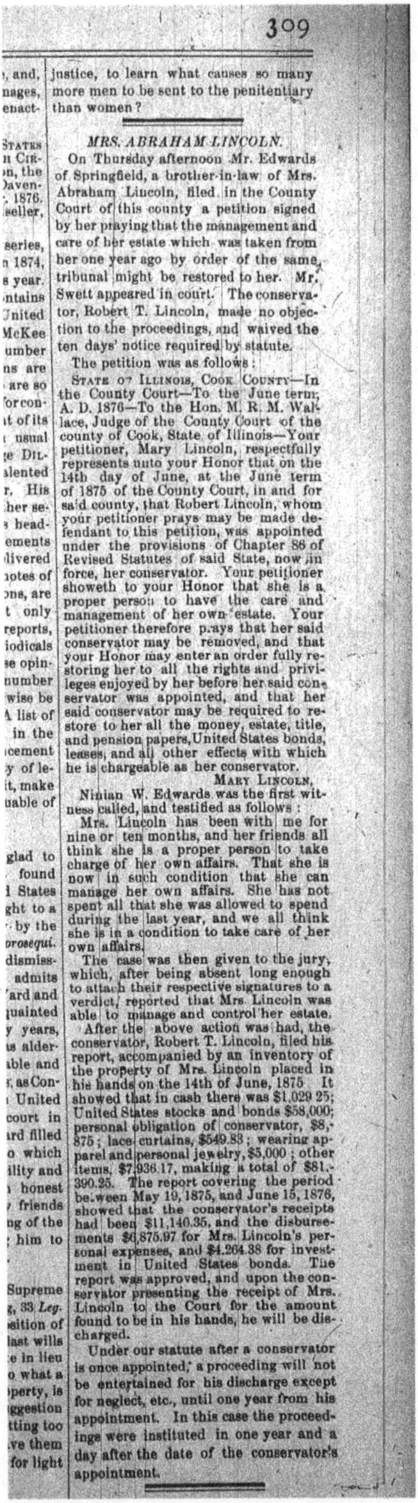

309

justice, to learn what causes so many more men to be sent to the penitentiary than women?

MRS. ABRAHAM LINCOLN.

On Thursday afternoon Mr. Edwards of Springfield, a brother-in-law of Mrs. Abraham Lincoln, filed in the County Court of this county a petition signed by her praying that the management and care of her estate which was taken from her one year ago by order of the same tribunal might be restored to her. Mr. Swett appeared in court. The conservator, Robert T. Lincoln, made no objection to the proceedings, and waived the ten days' notice required by statute.

The petition was as follows:

STATE OF ILLINOIS, COOK COUNTY—In the County Court—To the June term, A. D. 1876—To the Hon. M. R. M. Wallace, Judge of the County Court of the county of Cook, State of Illinois—Your petitioner, Mary Lincoln, respectfully represents unto your Honor that on the 14th day of June, at the June term of 1875 of the County Court, in and for said county, that Robert Lincoln, whom your petitioner prays may be made defendant to this petition, was appointed under the provisions of Chapter 86 of Revised Statutes of said State, now in force, her conservator. Your petitioner showeth to your Honor that she is a proper person to have the care and management of her own estate. Your petitioner therefore prays that her said conservator may be removed, and that your Honor may enter an order fully restoring her to all the rights and privileges enjoyed by her before her said conservator was appointed, and that her said conservator may be required to restore to her all the money, estate, title, and pension papers, United States bonds, leases, and all other effects with which he is chargeable as her conservator.

MARY LINCOLN.

Ninian W. Edwards was the first witness called, and testified as follows:

Mrs. Lincoln has been with me for nine or ten months, and her friends all think she is a proper person to take charge of her own affairs. That she is now in such condition that she can manage her own affairs. She has not spent all that she was allowed to spend during the last year, and we all think she is in a condition to take care of her own affairs.

The case was then given to the jury, which, after being absent long enough to attach their respective signatures to a verdict, reported that Mrs. Lincoln was able to manage and control her estate.

After the above action was had, the conservator, Robert T. Lincoln, filed his report, accompanied by an inventory of the property of Mrs. Lincoln placed in his hands on the 14th of June, 1875. It showed that in cash there was $1,029 25; United States stocks and bonds $58,000; personal obligation of conservator, $8,875; lace curtains, $549.83; wearing apparel and personal jewelry, $5,000; other items, $7,936.17, making a total of $81,390.25. The report covering the period between May 19, 1875, and June 15, 1876, showed that the conservator's receipts had been $11,140.35, and the disbursements $6,875.97 for Mrs. Lincoln's personal expenses, and $4,264.38 for investment in United States bonds. The report was approved, and upon the conservator presenting the receipt of Mrs. Lincoln to the Court for the amount found to be in his hands, he will be discharged.

Under our statute after a conservator is once appointed, a proceeding will not be entertained for his discharge except for neglect, etc., until one year from his appointment. In this case the proceedings were instituted in one year and a day after the date of the conservator's appointment.

f. David L. Phillips, editor, publisher, and co-owner of the *Illinois State Journal* newspaper from 1862 to 1878.

The article from the June 17, 1876, issue of Myra Bradwell's *Chicago Legal News* reporting on Mary Lincoln's second trial and verdict in which she was "restored to reason." The report was a reprint of a *Chicago Times* article, with the addition of a paragraph explaining the legal process to remove a conservator.

Needless to say there was no "writing up." My grandparents felt that there had been undesirable notoriety enough and were only too glad to retire from the public gaze.

They had no quarrel with Robert Lincoln. Convinced from the start that Mrs. Lincoln should have been allowed to remain at liberty, they combated the conditions that placed her in an insane hospital, but having done all they could to procure her release and having lived to see her again free, they were satisfied.

However, in view of the statements in Mary Lincoln's first letter to my grandmother after she had been declared of sound mind, it is interesting to read a note of Abraham Lincoln's to Joshua Speed.[g]

"This one," wrote Mary Lincoln, "as my beloved husband always said, was so very different from the rest of us."

And her husband, writing to Speed in Oct. 1846 (I quote from Ida M. Tarbell's *In the Footsteps of the Lincolns*), said,

> Bob is short and low and I expect always will be. He talks very plainly, almost as plainly as anybody. He is quite smart enough. I sometimes fear he is one of the little rare-ripe sort that are smarter at about five than ever after.[h] He has a great deal of that sort of mischief that is the offspring of such animal spirits. Since I began this letter a messenger came to tell me that Bob is lost, but by the time I reached the house his mother had found him and had whipped him and by now, very likely, he has run away again.[10]

In her next letter to my grandfather Mrs. Lincoln appears to be chiefly worried over the title to the house she formerly owned in Chicago, although she does take occasion to criticize Swett for a letter to her brother-in-law.[i]

Springfield, Ill.
June 22nd, 1876

Judge Bradwell:

My dear friend:

Swett has written a letter to Mr. Edwards, which has been received this morning, filled with the most voluminous falsehoods.

g. Speed was a close friend of Lincoln's in Springfield, as well as Lincoln's roommate when both men were bachelors.

h. Pritchard views this comment as negative toward Robert—as have most Lincoln biographers, especially William Herndon. Herndon, who disliked Robert for multiple reasons, once declared in an oblique reference to this statement that Abraham Lincoln often said of his children, "These children may be something sometimes, if they are not merely rare-ripes, rotten ripes, hothouse plants. I have always noticed that a rare-ripe child quickly matures, but rots as quickly."[9]

i. Swett had claimed the house title was unclear and in litigation (unfortunately, no letters or records exist to explain why). Mary perceived his statement as proof of some conspiracy to deprive her of her monthly payments. That Mary suffered paranoia over losing this monthly income, and a continued delusion that Robert was intent to defraud her, is obvious. Besides instructing James Bradwell to investigate the matter, Ninian Edwards mentioned it to Leonard Swett twice in two days and wrote Robert that Mary was "afraid" that he would not pay, while banker Jacob Bunn none too subtly informed Robert that he now had power of attorney over Mary's bonds and the power to collect the rent. Judge Bradwell must have found nothing wrong with the title, as no letters from him about it have been found, although according to Mary he did not think it a good arrangement. For his part, Robert fully repaid his mother for the house, making the final payment more than four months early, in Dec. 1880.[11]

Amongst other things Swett writes that the title to the house 375 West Wash. St. is in litigation, the title being imperfect. You remember well the article I showed you, which R. T. Lincoln drew up, in regard to *this* house which I gave him subject to the rent to be paid for seven years, from the time I deeded it to him.[j] It is evident that after these long years it is rather late for a flaw to be in the lease.

May I employ your services to examine this lease. It is evidently gotten up to prevent the monthly payment of the rent. *Ascertain correctly* and write me all the facts in the case. The lease was examined and considered perfect at the time of the purchase. It was purchased from a man by the name of Cook, who resides near Batavia, Ill. I presume the people who reside in the same block feel very easy as to *their* titles, Cook, building all the houses.

There is beyond question the most unmitigated villainy in the case. Do not delay an hour, my dear Judge Bradwell—in regard to this involving such a loss—It appears that I must see yourself and Mrs. Bradwell. Pardon blots and everything. Fail me not—at once write.

Your friend,
Mary Lincoln.[12]

Mrs. Lincoln, in her next letter, complains that "[n]one of my treasures, in the way of rich and rare presentations that were made me, have been returned to me."[k]

Presumably she refers to the trunks and tin bond box which she had requested many times during her son's conservatorship, for it was a matter of common knowledge in my family and among others familiar with Mary Lincoln that her personal treasures and mementoes were kept in these containers. It is of court record that Robert Lincoln was authorized to send these to his mother the previous December but, apparently, did not do so.[l]

This letter in which she makes this complaint is given below:

j. See chapter 7, annotation g.

k. On June 19, 1876, Mary had written to her son, "Do not fail to send me without *the least* delay, *all* my paintings, Moses in the bulrushes included—also the fruit picture, which hung in your dining room—my silver set with large silver waiter presented me by New York friends, my silver tete-a-tete set also other articles your wife appropriated and which are *well known* to you, must be sent, without a day's delay. Two lawyers and myself, have just been together and their list, coincides with my own and will be published in a few days. . . . Send me my laces, my diamonds, my jewelry—My unmade silks, white lace dress—double lace shawl and flounce, lace scarf—2 black shawls—one black lace deep flounce, white lace sets ½ yd in width and eleven yards in length. . . . Send me all I have written for, you have tried your game of robbery long enough."[13] Ninian Edwards and Leonard Swett—acting as legal representatives for Mary and Robert Lincoln respectively—thereafter had a long and detailed correspondence about Mary's demands and accusations of thievery by Robert and his wife concerning the widow's "treasures and mementoes." Edwards presented his sister-in-law's demands, but always while assuring Swett that he and his wife did not believe Robert had done or was doing anything improper. Robert was "surprised and pained" by his mother's claims and allegations; Leonard Swett was irate. He told Edwards that everything Mary named as having been "stolen" had been in reality a gift to her son and daughter-in-law, and the letters she wrote full of demands were "such as none but an insane mother would write to her son." Swett and Robert therefore decided not to return anything "demanded as a matter of right, accompanied with the assertion that they were obtained improperly." Swett also declared that if Mary Lincoln did not desist from her demands and threats of lawsuits against Robert that he would "irrespective of Robert or anyone . . . have her confined as an insane person, whatever may be the clamor or consequences."[14] Mary's threats thereafter ceased.

l. See chapter 7, annotations h and i.

Springfield, Ill.,
July 7th, 1876.

My dear Mrs. Bradwell:

I have received no letter from you, am I forgotten? If you ascertain any facts in relation to 375 West Wash. St. please inform me.

A weak "invention of the enemy" united with villainous falsehood. That Swett, should become so debased as to try and drag down to his own debased standard the son of the noblest, most honest man, who has ever lived. None of my treasures, in the way of rich and rare presentations that were made me, have been returned to me. As I truly told R. T. L. villains could not venture to approach my dearly beloved husband in the other world. *His* reply I gave you.

My husband always told me that he only liked those whom I did and when I remembered the contrast between R. T. L. and my other blessed sons, the latter so lovely, gentle and noble, and my darling husband who worshipped me so greatly, that often he said that I was his weakness.

We conversed very unreservedly together when you [were] in S. (Springfield). Anything you said to me will be held sacred. Some little communications I made you *please* breathe to no living soul. We discussed Prof. S. (Rev. David Swing)[m] who between ourselves I think amounts to very little. (The subject of Mrs. E. [Edwards] do please erase from you[r] memory, as an honorable woman.) I entreat you to cast *all thoughts* of either of these persons from your mind or *mention*.

What are your plans? Believe me, I am deeply interested in them, for the next six weeks or two months. Write me dear friend, when you receive this scrawl, I am so anxious to hear from you. My pen is refusing its office, so I must bid you adieu, until I hear from you. Please present my love to all your family whilst I remain

Your very affectionate friend
Mary Lincoln.[16]

m. Reverend David Swing, a Presbyterian minister in Chicago. While Mary was friends with Swing and his wife, Elizabeth, since 1866, their relationship grew much closer after Tad's death in 1871, to the point that Mary showered the Swing children with gifts. The vindictive tone of this statement about Swing comes from his August 1875 newspaper editorial defending Robert Lincoln's actions in regard to Mary.[15]

Reverend David Swing. Reprinted from Frederick William Gookin, *The Chicago Literary Club: A History of Its First Fifty Years* (Chicago: Printed for the Club, 1926), 124.

Mrs. Lincoln's resentment is still strong in the last letter she ever wrote my grandmother in this country. Her son and Swett still appear as "scoundrels," and she continues to be worried about the condition of the West Washington Street property.

Her reference to the sail "down the bay" concerns her proposed trip to Europe.

Springfield, Ill.
July 14, '76

My dear Mrs. Bradwell:

Your expected letter has been received. As to the abstract, I suppose R. T. L. has it. Mr. Cook from whom 375 West Wash St. was purchased, resides somewhere in the country, near Chicago, doubtless transacts business in the latter place.

Mr. Phillips made me a very pleasant call a few evenings since. Is very vehement against two of the greatest scoundrels of the age R. T. L. and Swett. The last of whom he pronounces a very profligate man and says that my husband had become thoroughly disgusted with S. (Swett) and so expressed himself to P. (Phillips) Certainly as the wife I heard enough against S. (Swett).

We speak of you so frequently. Would that we could daily meet, converse together. Will not Judge Bradwell return west by the way of Springfield? I, so much wish to see him before the sail, "down the bay." If you still have Mrs. Ellen Johnson (colored) address—please forward it to me—also, please drop her a note to call to see you—as she would like to hear—that a *faithful, devoted* son failed in his attempt to render a deeply bereaved mother *insane. Do* see her for my sake, my dear friend.

Will write you soon again. My sister is well and cheerful—Too much kindness of heart is the only trouble of the *other party.* I assure you—easily imposed upon an innocent by those who make a representation of want of means. Others justly require what is

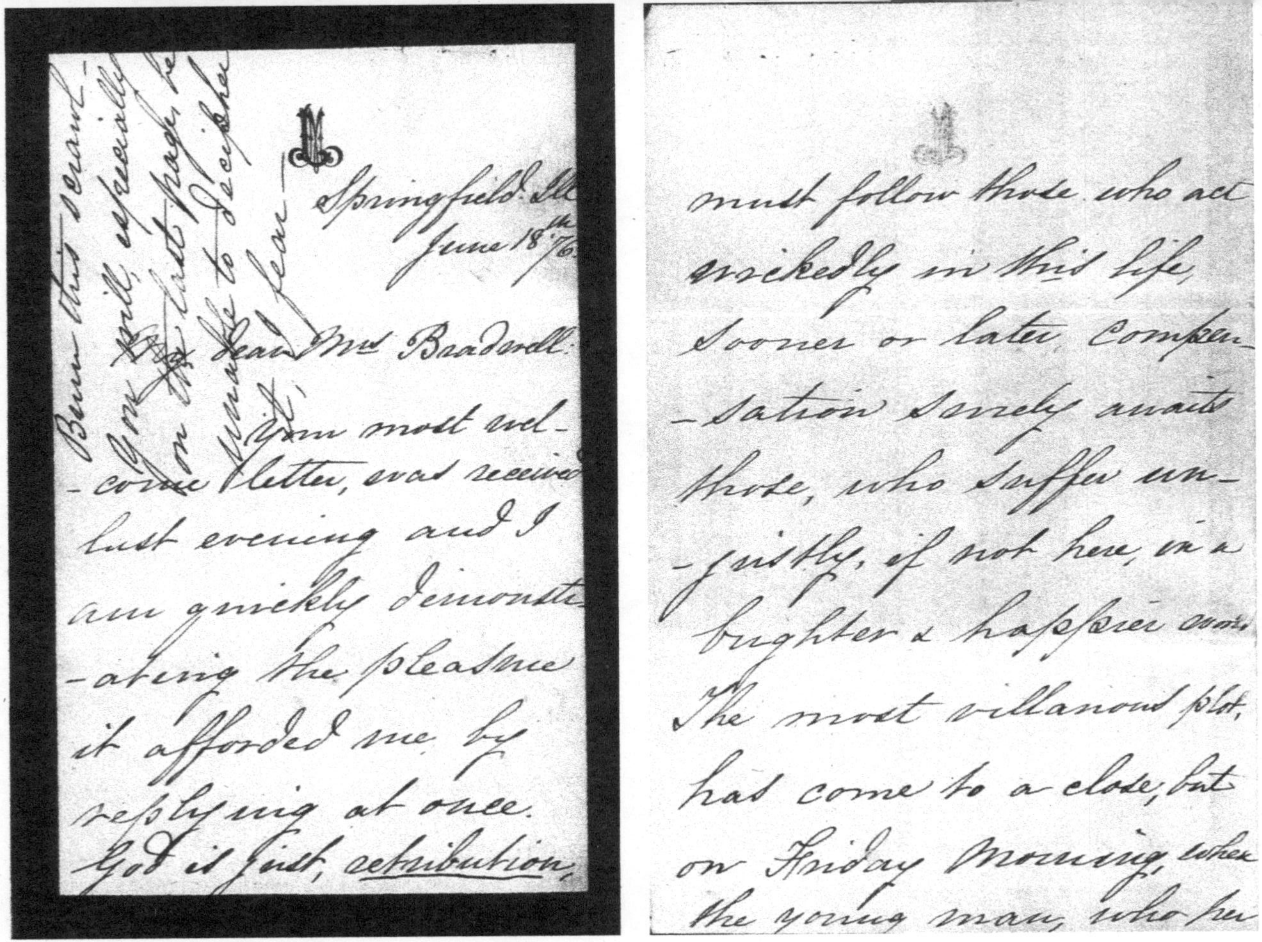

Springfield Ill
June 18th 76

My dear Mrs Bradwell:
Your most wel-
-come letter, was received
last evening and I
am quickly demonstr-
-ating the pleasure
it afforded me by
replying at once.
God is just, retribution,

Burn this second -
I am ill, especially
on the last page, be
unable to decipher
it, I fear -

must follow those who act
wickedly in this life,
sooner or later, compen-
-sation surely awaits
those, who suffer un-
-justly, if not here, in a
brighter & happier world.
The most villanous plot,
has come to a close; but
on Friday Morning, when
the young man, who her

First two pages of Mary Lincoln's June 18, 1876, letter to Myra Bradwell, in which the former First Lady vilifies her son for his perceived "villainous plot" to steal her money. Courtesy Library of Congress.

thus bestowed. Much love to you and yours. Write and do not act *quite so mean* by your silence.

Affectionately yours,
M.L.[17]

In the latter part of July 1876, my grandmother visited Mrs. Lincoln at Springfield at the latter's urgent invitation. For the next few years Mrs. Lincoln spent much of her time abroad, and the letters which she sent to my grandmother during this period were ones of retrospection and reminiscence. They are beautiful, calm letters, as different from those of the early and middle seventies as a quiet sea after a storm.

Robert T. Lincoln and Leonard Swett, whom Mary Lincoln characterized as "two of the greatest scoundrels of the age." Robert Lincoln photo courtesy Friends of Hildene, Inc. Leonard Swett photo from Frederick Francis Cook, *Bygone Days of Chicago* (Chicago: A. C. McClurg, 1910), 324, used courtesy University of Illinois at Urbana-Champaign, http://www.archive.org/stream/bygonedaysinchicoocook#page/324/mode/2up.

9

In the fall of 1876 Mary Todd Lincoln took up her residence in France, where she found the peace and tranquility that had been denied her.[a] During this period her letters to my grandparents were in a calmly sympathetic vein, in striking contrast to the wrathful accusatory missives in which she charged her son, Robert T. Lincoln, with incarcerating her in an insane asylum to obtain her estate.

Only one, the first, contains any apparent reference to that phase of her life. This letter is dated Dec. 1, 1876:

Pau, France.

My dear Mrs. Bradwell:

You have been so frequently in my thoughts of late that I feel that I must give vent to them in words which will be but a faint expression of the love and gratitude I feel towards you. When we parted in Springfield last summer I scarcely thought it possible that we would not again meet, ere my departure across the waters, but such has been the case, but that will be no reason that we cannot frequently hear from each other. I think often of you leading the occupied life you do yet sweetened by the presence of your devoted husband and two most interesting children[b] filling your home with so much happiness.

Your daughter I suppose still remains at school destined to become one of the most learned young ladies in our country.[c] Kiss her sweet face for me and tell her that she must not apply herself

9

a. Mary left Springfield in September 1876 to go to Europe. Supposedly she told her sister Elizabeth that she could no longer endure the fact that all her family and friends considered her insane. "I feel it in their soothing manner. If I should say the moon is made of green cheese they would heartily and smilingly agree with me," Mary said.[1] She also left the country "for self protection" she said, for fear that her son would have her recommitted.[2] Elizabeth Edwards told Robert Lincoln, "her resentful nature found it necessary to place the ocean between you and herself." Mary traveled with her nephew, Edward Lewis Baker Jr. to New York, where she sailed for Havre, France. From Havre she traveled to Pau, the city she previously visited during her 1868–71 European tour, which became her main residence for the next four years. "I go an exile, and alone!," she lamented to her sister when they parted.[3]

b. Daughter Bessie and son James.

c. Bessie Bradwell was an eighteen-year-old student at Northwestern Law School in 1876. She ultimately graduated as class valedictorian.

too much to her books.[d] Doubtless she enjoyed her visit east very much. Did you visit the Centennial?

I believe I told you that I had already some friends residing at Pau.[e] They received me with the greatest affection and I have made some new acquaintances whom I like very much but if I could *only* see you, dear precious friend, this day, not to speak of your dear noble husband, I will allow myself to dwell on so pleasant a picture. This place is very beautiful to me surrounded by the Pyrenees whose distant peaks are already covered with snow. I sleep under *four* soft blankets, the air growing a little *cool*, yet, during my six weeks stay, I have never heard the least wind. One of the peculiarities I am told of the climate.

The drives, are simply enchanting, two days since I drove out six miles to Gau and returned, and the lovely Chateaus built upon the hills all facing the mountains I cannot attempt to describe clearly. I am situated at one of the finest hotels, most accommodating landlord, very near the chateau of Henry 4th[f] where I frequently wander through the grand rooms, so filled with historical interest, and beyond a park of miles—with seats under the beautiful old trees.

Close your doors some day, my bright appreciative friend, take your husband's arm, bring your talented daughter and son with you and rest. I have received some delightful letters from friends, and some most distinguished ones who dwell in this land and most of them are natives, who give me so cordial a welcome to their shores. On my table, lies a card received today from a gentleman and his wife who reside at Pau. An Austrian, Baron de Brenneke,[g] who was in Washington while we were there. They often visit me and are very accomplished people—plain and *so elegant* and consequently so unassuming. I fear that I am wearying you with so long a letter.

Would that I could see you again but I am allowed tranquility here and am not harassed by a *demon*.[h] I wrote Mrs. Ellen Johnson 1425 Butterfield St. recently a letter. *Will you* see her. Do write me without the least delay. I am very anxious to hear from you.

d. Mary Lincoln, whose life was filled with tragedy and sorrow, suffered from a depressed and dismal outlook on the vagaries of life. She liked to tell young women to have fun and not be too serious, lest they miss out on laughter and gaiety. As she once wrote her daughter-in-law, Mary Harlan Lincoln, "You should go out *every day* and enjoy yourself—you are so *very young* and should be gay as a lark. Trouble comes soon enough, my dear child, and you must enjoy life, whenever you can."[4]

e. It is unknown exactly who these friends were.

f. Chateau de Pau, birthplace of Henry IV of France in 1553.

g. Probably a misspelling of Le Baron de Bennecker, a government officer in Pau.[5]

h. This refers to her son, Robert Lincoln.

Remember me to the Judge. *Always* your affectionate, *deeply* grateful friend.

Mary Lincoln

Write and tell me everything. M.L.[6]

Despite her residence abroad, Mrs. Lincoln retained her grasp of political affairs at home. In April 1877, she wrote my grandmother, urging Judge Bradwell to seek a place on the United States Supreme Court bench and commenting on General Logan's political ambitions.

Pau, France
Basses, Pyrenees.
April 12th, 1877

My dear Mrs. Bradwell:

It has been some time since I had the pleasure of receiving your most welcome letter yet, notwithstanding the lapse of *time*, you have been frequently in my thoughts and most fondly remembered. I have been much saddened within the last two months with hearing from my sister Mrs. Edwards of the loss of two sweet little grandchildren, one, the only child of Charles Edwards, a very bright promising little girl and Albert, the other brother, has lost a little girl—both with scarlet fever. Naturally, it has cast a great gloom over their households.

When you wrote me you had just returned from Springfield and Gen. Logan[i] was in a state of great suspense. I suppose he consoles himself with the hope of the possible *future* presidency. Speaking of these things, my dear friend, why is it with your husband's great legal ability, noble heart, and name, why do you not turn your attention to securing *that* place on the Supreme Bench at Washington for him.[j] You with your great talents and diplomacy, could so well arrange affairs. Judge B. is far too modest for the age in which he lives, and so much care and work would be spared him by the *change*. A wife can do so much for her husband which you have undoubtedly done. It would gratify me so much to have

i. John A. Logan of Illinois. Logan was a lawyer and Democrat politician in his early years. He fought in the Union army from 1862 to 1865 during the Civil War, and mustered out as a major general of volunteers. Logan became a Republican after the war and was elected to the U.S House of Representatives in 1867, where he served until his election to the U.S. Senate in 1871. Logan's "state of great suspense" in April 1877 was his attempt at a Cabinet position or a foreign appointment from new president Rutherford B. Hayes, which was unsuccessful. Two years later he was elected to the U.S. Senate from Illinois again, and reelected in 1885. In 1884 he sought the Republican presidential nomination. He lost to James G. Blaine but became Blaine's running mate.

j. Associate Justice David Davis—who had been appointed to the seat by President Lincoln in 1862—resigned from the U.S. Supreme Court in March 1877 after his election to the U.S. Senate. President Rutherford B. Hayes nominated John Marshall Harlan in October 1877 to fill the vacancy.

that *vacant* place assigned him. I believe a few quiet words would secure it. You know how greatly I prize you both and what an interest I take in you and yours.

When you see Mrs. Ellen Johnson please say to her that I wrote her in Nov. last and not a line have I yet received from her. I suppose your dear daughter (to whom [I] present much love) still continues in college. Only a very great man will be her husband, be assured. I hope soon to hear from you. Please address me by name and write "Poste Restante" on left hand corner. Remember me to the Judge. I remain your affectionate friend

Mary Lincoln[7]

I write this very hastily. My address is Mrs. Abraham Lincoln, Pau, Basse Pyrennes, France.

Her next letter was written in Sorrento, Italy.

Sorrento, Italy[k]
April 22, 1878

My dear Mrs. Bradwell:

In the quiet of this beautiful place, I have been thinking a good deal of you and have concluded to inflict a letter upon you, so that I, too, may not be entirely forgotten by yourself and the Judge. A few weeks since, I came round by sea, from Marseilles to Naples, and as it was my second visit to the latter place within the last few years, I remained there only a week, but will return there in a few days.

It is my season of sadness[l] and Naples with its noise, was unendurable. With guide book in my hands, some years since I had visited all places that were considered to be of interest, and it is well for me that I did so for I could not interest myself *now* as I did *then*, in visiting each place. My heart was then filled with great sorrow, but since that time the crushing hand of bereavement has been laid so heavily upon me, that it is only by a strong effort of will that I revisit places.[m]

k. Mary spent two months in Italy in early 1878 visiting Naples, Rome, and Sorrento. Practically nothing is known of that trip. Only three letters during that period are previously published, all to Mary's banker and mostly about financial matters. This is the first known letter from Sorrento and the first known detailed account of her actions and thoughts in Italy.[8]

l. Springtime: her sons Eddie and Willie both died in February, and her husband was murdered in April.

m. It is clear from this letter and others that however improved mentally Mary Lincoln was during her European exile, she still suffered from depression. Only one week after this letter to Myra Bradwell, Mary wrote a similar sentiment to her banker, Jacob Bunn, from Naples: "I find the climate of Italy very soft and pleasant; having visited here once before, in former years, prevents the feeling of novelty, yet as sorrowful as I *then* was, my grief has been greatly *intensified since*, consequently, I take no interest whatever in fresh scenes and objects."[9] Mary's depressed state was discovered by the *New York Star* newspaper, which published a gossipy article around this time declaring the widow was leading "a secluded life in an interior town in France" and that "she still indulges in her propensity for buying things for which she has no use, and filling closets with articles wholly unnecessary." The article was reprinted across the U.S., causing the *Springfield* [Ill.] *State Journal* to rebut the accusation, stating that while Mary was living in Pau, "the fact that she is in almost weekly cordial and intelligent correspondence with her friends in this city, would indicate that the rest of the story is without foundation."[10]

I went to Herculaneum,[n] before I left Naples also to the "Castle of St. Elmo."[o] Stopped at the Hotel de Rupie which commands the finest view of Vesuvius and the Bay of Naples but nothing equals, I think, the charming scenery of Sorrento. Even Mrs. Stowe's imaginative pen has scarcely done it justice.[p] In front of my Hotel in full view lies a grand chain of mountains, Vesuvius, rising above them all. The Bay in full view, an orange and lemon grove within these grounds, trees bowed down with their fruit, of so much larger size and better flavor than we have with us. The villa of Aristides was the sole object of interest to me at Herculaneum.

Close up some day your dear daughter's books, bring her to these lands, so filled with historical associations, have the Judge accompany you for a rest and you will find yourselves, so well repaid, for your journey. My beloved husband and myself for hours would sit down and anticipate the pleasant time, we would have in *quietly* visiting places and in *halting* at such spots as this, when his official labors were ended. God works in such a mysterious way and we are left to bow to His will. But to some of us, *resignation* will never come. But perhaps for the tears shed *here*, compensation will succeed the grief of the *present time.*[q]

Would that I could see you all once more, for you are very dear to my heart. My sister, Mrs. Edwards, writes me quite frequently and today I have written her a long letter. When you receive this letter, dear Mrs. Bradwell, sit down and write me a long one in reply. Please remember me to your family. If you remember you are owing me a letter. What has become of Mrs. Ellen Johnson? She was a faithful friend to me and I hope she is doing well. I wrote her a year since and have received no reply. I miss her good washing. I assure you when you see her remember me to her. Tell her I have a whole trunk of clothes for her, she will understand. Do write my dear friend.

Direct to Pau, France Basses Pyrenees.

Poste Restante

Always your affectionate friend

Mary Lincoln[12]

n. An ancient Roman resort town buried in lava in 79 A.D. from the eruption of Mt. Vesuvius that also buried Pompeii. It was discovered, in a state of preservation, in the late eighteenth century and excavated.

o. A fourteenth-century castle in Naples, Italy.

p. Harriet Beecher Stowe wrote a romantic novel, *Agnes of Sorrento*, in 1861.

q. Mary's letter, so full of pathos and pain at a life lost and dreams devastated, is redolent of a poem about Sorrento by a similarly dispirited John Addington Symonds, published in 1880—a poem eerily similar to Mary Lincoln's feelings and situation, and one it is not inconceivable that Mary, a great lover of literature and especially poetry, may have read:

> Love was the wand I swayed at will:
> Not Ischia's slope nor Capri's hill
> Have joys so fair and free,
> As in that brief enchanted spring
> From every humble household thing
> I fashioned for my glee.
>
> Too soon it fled; and year by year
> Came slowly trooping care and fear
> Spent powers and clouded faith:
> A sorrow to my spirit clung—
> A pang, not mine, whose poison stung
> The soul it could not scathe.
>
> Nor health nor hope remained; I fled
> From land to land; my weary head
> In strangers' homes I laid:
> And now, by fair Sorrento's bay,
> I sit and sigh this sweet spring day,
> Beneath the olive shade.[11]

In June she returned to Pau, where she learned my grandmother was en route to Europe to visit her.

Pau, France
July 4, 1878

My dear Mrs. Bradwell:

Your letter of July 2nd is just this *moment* received. I am greatly surprised that you have not received the letter I wrote you, at least *ten* days since from Vichy,[r] in reply to your *most* welcome one, dated Chicago, making the pleasant announcement that you were to sail for Europe, on the 12th of June.[s] I addressed the letter to the care of Mrs. Walker,[t] Beverly, England. You did not give me the name of your hotel. Please enquire at the post office at Beverly for it.

I am so anxious to see you and would go anywhere to meet you, but have been laid up in bed for the last two days with boils under my left arm. Address me *Poste Restante* Pau, France. I find on my return the usual beautiful hotel closed for the summer season where I have stopped but am in plain comfortable quarters at Hotel de l' Europe. I cannot contain myself this solitary 4th of July, knowing that you are *so near* and yet *so far*. It cannot be that you are not to receive the letters I write you, my *very very* dear friend. The Vichy waters did me no good. However, I was not very much in need of them.

Write me at once. I cannot do anything today. My thoughts are so much with you.

Very affectionately your friend
Mary Lincoln[14]

Although apparently in great pain, Mrs. Lincoln continues to write tenderly of her affection for my grandmother.

r. A spa and resort town in central France, near Clermont-Ferrand.

s. Myra Bradwell sailed from New York on the steamship *Abyssinia* of the Cunard Line on June 12 for Liverpool, England, where she arrived on June 22.[13]

t. Uncertain. There is a Mrs. George Walker mentioned in an 1871 letter (Turner and Turner, *Mary Todd Lincoln*, 136, 590). Mrs. Walker was a daughter of Rhoda (Mrs. James W.) White, who was a friend of Mary's during the White House years.

Pau, France,
July 6th 1878

My dear Mrs. Bradwell:

By this time you must be receiving my frequent letters. In looking over your last letter, I perceive that the date is June 27th. I wrote you on the 4th of July. Where are you now? An Englishman told me on yesterday that Beverly was in Yorkshire, consequently not so near London as I had supposed.

Vichy waters, have brought out several disagreeable boils under my left arm and the pain extends over my whole body. With the *very very* warm weather we are having, I am not spending a very pleasant time.

Do write me at once my dear friend. I am so anxious to hear from you, you are well aware how near you are to my heart. You have no friend, I believe, who loves you *half* so well as myself. I write with difficulty owing to the pain.

Affectionately yours
Mary Lincoln[15]

Shortly after the letter I give below was written, my grandmother arrived at Pau and spent some time with Mrs. Lincoln.

Pau, France
July 19, 1878

My dear Mrs. Bradwell:

This morning's mail brought me an envelope enclosing two letters for yourself from Beverly. Of course, I will retain them until you arrive. I cannot express to you, with what pleasure I look forward to *your* coming. I hope when you receive this letter, your health will have improved. I fear with your indisposition you have seen very little of London. However, *in the future*, you have time enough for it all.

A view of Pau, Pyrenees, France, the town in which Mary Lincoln lived during most of her European exile from 1876 to 1880. Photo courtesy Library of Congress, call number: LOT 13418, no. 416.

It is a pity you did not bring your very sweet and interesting daughter over with you. I am longing greatly to see you, my very dear friend and I am sure you will feel anxious for your two letters—when you write to your dear noble husband, please present my kindest regards. I feel very tenderly attached to yourself and family—*the intolerable heat* prevents my inflicting a long letter upon you. When you come, we will direct our way very soon to the beautiful Pyrenees.[u] Four hours by sail brings us to the heart of them. I trust a breeze is refreshing you this morning, which *Pau* does not dream of. Do write me at once. Ever yours, most affectionately

Mary Lincoln[18]

After my grandmother returned to the United States, Mary Lincoln continued to correspond with her, but these later letters add nothing to the record I have sought to perpetuate here. They are sweet, chatty letters of her travels and her friends. In none of them does she mention the gray days of the past, and to publish them would, I think, be inexcusable prying into Mary Todd Lincoln's intimate affairs.[v] Surely, in life, she was permitted little enough privacy.

She returned to this country in October 1880, and whatever malignant fate pursued her seems to have selected her homecoming for one more hostile gesture, another turning of the barbs of sorrow and neglect that had been thrust so deeply into her heart.[w]

The *New York Sun* wrote at some length of her arrival, and because I have rarely read anything so pathetic, I quote a part of the account here.

When the *Amerique* reached New York a throng was assembled on the dock and a greater throng was in the street outside the gates. During the tedious process of working the ship into her dock, there was a great crush in that part of the vessel where the gang plank was to be swung. Among the passengers who were here gathered was an aged lady. She was dressed plainly. Her face was furrowed, and her hair was streaked with white. This was the widow of Abraham Lincoln. She was almost unnoticed. She had

u. It is unclear when Myra Bradwell reached Mary Lincoln at Pau or for how long the two friends visited. A *Chicago Tribune* society page story reported on August 18 that Bradwell had "reached Paris," but gives no further details.[16] It also is unclear when Myra Bradwell left Europe to return to America; the only discovered notice of such was from more than one year later, October 1879.[17] This raises the question of whether Myra Bradwell spent more than one year across the ocean—highly unlikely—or if she returned to Europe on a separate trip in 1879. If the latter, she may have visited her friend Mary Lincoln a second time. Unfortunately, there is no known evidence of a second visit, and Pritchard does not mention it in her manuscript.

v. These letters have not been found, and their dates are unknown.

w. By 1880, Mary's physical maladies of headaches, bodily pains, neuralgia, incontinence, and severe cough were compounded by a much more serious affliction. In Dec. 1879, she fell off a stool while hanging a painting and seriously injured her spine, causing her intense pain on her left side and difficulty walking. The doctors set her back in plasters, but this did not alleviate the suffering of what she referred to as her "*almost* broken back." Then in June 1880, due to the pain and weakness in her left side, Mary fell down a flight of stairs, further injuring her back, which the doctor set in plasters once again. After four years of exile, and now lonely and in great pain, Mary Lincoln decided to go home.[19]

> come alone across the ocean, but a nephew met her at quarantine. She had spent the last four years in the South of France. When the gang plank was finally swung aboard, Mme. Bernhardt[x] and her companions, including Mme. Columbier of the troupe, were the first to descend. The fellow voyagers of the actress pressed about her to bid adieu, and a cheer was raised which turned her head and provoked an astonished smile as she stepped upon the wharf. The gates were besieged and there was some difficulty in bringing in the carriage, which was to convey the actress to the hotel. She temporarily waited in the freight office at the entrance to the wharf. Mrs. Lincoln, leaning on the arm of her nephew,[y] walked toward the gate. A policeman touched the aged lady on the shoulder and bade her stand back. She retreated with her nephew into the line of spectators, while Manager Abbey's carriage was slowly brought in. Mme. Bernhardt was handed in and the carriage made its way out through a mass of struggling longshoremen and idlers who pressed about it, and stared in at the open windows. After it, went out the others, who had been passengers on the *Amerique*, Mrs. Lincoln among the rest.[20] [z]

There is little more to say. In this series I have tried to present a phase of Mary Todd Lincoln's life, heretofore untold, a dark chapter that should, I think, be universally known. If these old letters and their attendant documents bring belated understanding of Mary Todd Lincoln, her trials and her sorrows, then I am happy, happier than I can say.

Mary Lincoln went back to Springfield, back to the house in which she became Lincoln's bride, where she died July 16, 1882.[aa] A strange figure, a high-strung, tragic figure destined to know heartache and sorrow and misunderstanding only too well. If this heritage from my grandparents has explained away some of the latter, I am content.

x. Actress Sarah Bernhardt.

y. Edward Lewis Baker Jr., grandson of Elizabeth and Ninian Edwards.

z. Mary sailed from Havre, France, aboard the steamer *L'Amerique* on Oct. 15, 1880. During the twelve-day journey across the Atlantic, the celebrated actress Sarah Bernhardt famously saved Mary from falling head first down a stairway. "You might have been killed, Madame," Bernhardt said. "'Yes,' [Mary] answered with a sigh of regret, 'but it was not God's will.'" Bernhardt then realized that "I had just done this unhappy woman the only service I ought not to have done her—I had saved her from death."[21]

aa. Mary's death at age sixty-three was most likely from a stroke. Some physician-historians have theorized Mary's final illness and death occurred, at least in part, from untreated diabetes. This diagnosis was made from her symptoms of urinary incontinence, current attacks of boils, and dramatic weight loss beginning in 1879. Dr. W. A. Evans, in his landmark psychological (and to some extent physiological) study of Mary Lincoln, suspected Mary suffered a diabetic coma during the final week of her life and died of stroke, "probably due to the rupture of a blood vessel in the brain." Mary's body was laid out in the parlor of the Edwards home—the same room in which she married Abraham Lincoln—and her funeral held in the First Presbyterian Church of Springfield. She was buried next to her husband in the Lincoln tomb in Oak Ridge Cemetery.[22]

EDITOR'S EPILOGUE

There were many occurrences in Mary Lincoln's life between her return to the United States in October 1880 and her death in July 1882 that Myra Pritchard omits but should be added to the story. The most relevant in regard to Pritchard's manuscript—and some would argue the most important overall—was Mary's reconciliation with her son Robert in 1881.

The day after Mary's June 18, 1876, letter to Myra Bradwell seeking vengeance on Robert (see chapter 8), Mary wrote her son a letter in which she called him a thief and demanded back all her property in his possession.[1] She then cut all ties to him for the next five years. In her letters during that time, Mary even refused to write out her son's name, only his initials or some malicious characterization such as a "demon" or a "monster of mankind." In 1877 Robert replied to a letter asking about his mother that she was "somewhere in Europe," but he did not know her address.[2] Robert would have written to his mother, he told his aunt in 1879, but he did not think such a missive would be well received. "If I could persuade myself otherwise, I would write to her at once and not think I was making any concession," he wrote, "for I have not allowed her anger at me to have any other effect upon me than regret that she should so feel and express herself towards me." Mary did, however, continually send gifts to her granddaughter Mamie, which gave Robert a hope that his mother's animosity toward him one day might end. "I am very anxious that it should," he wrote. "Its existence has been very distressing to me."[3]

As for Mary, she was not only angry and hurt by Robert; she also was afraid of him. By the time she was ready to sail for the United States in 1880, she feared to, thinking Robert would immediately have her arrested and recommitted. When he learned of this apprehension, Robert asked his aunt Elizabeth to assure his mother that "under no possible circumstances" would he do so. "I have no reason to think that such interference is now or will hereafter be proper but that whatever I might think hereafter, I would under no circumstance do anything," he stated. "If I could have foreseen my own experience in the matter, no consideration would have induced me to go through with it, the ordinary troubles and distresses of life are enough without such as that."[4]

Mary Lincoln returned to Springfield, Illinois, in 1880 to live again at the Edwards home. It was there, in May 1881, that she and Robert reconciled. Robert was at that time secretary of war under President James A. Garfield, and was on an official War Department trip to Fort Leavenworth, Kansas. He stopped in Springfield from May 26 to May 27 on his way west, and spoke to his mother for the first time since 1876. Tradition holds that Robert went on a personal visit and brought his daughter Mamie with him—Mary Lincoln's little namesake, whom she adored—as a way to help smooth the peace with his mother. This appears to be a case of historical hearsay, as no primary evidence exists to suggest it was true.[5] Exactly how the meeting was arranged is unknown, but it seems likely that Elizabeth Edwards had a hand in it. She was the mother figure who understood the stubborn Mary and the matriarch who respected Robert and always regretted the mother-son rift; she was probably the only person who *could have* reunited them. From then until Mary's death in July 1882, Robert and his family visited his mother every few weeks.

Robert and his wife also were great advocates of an increase in Mary Lincoln's government pension from three thousand dollars to five thousand. When Congress granted the widow of President Garfield the latter amount after his assassination in July 1881, Robert and Mary Harlan Lincoln helped Mary achieve her own increase by convincing influential businessman Cyrus Field to lobby Congress on her behalf, not only for a raise in her pension but also for interest and back payments on the difference.[6] To Mary the increase not only was fair but also brought back her delusions of poverty. By late 1881 her physical health was seriously declining and she claimed she could not afford the appropriate medical treatment. She suffered from inflammation of the spine, kidney trouble, terrible headaches, bodily swelling, and loss of eyesight. She needed assistance to walk and could not descend the stairs. Her doctor, world-renowned orthopedic physician and childhood friend Dr. Louis A. Sayre, announced to the press that Mary's annual three-thousand-dollar Congressional pension was inadequate to cover her necessary medical costs.[7]

U.S. House member William M. Springer also furthered her cause when he requested Sayre and three other eminent physicians—experts in ophthalmology, neurology, and kidney diseases—examine the widow's case and give a report of her physical condition to Congress.[8] The physicians declared she suffered from chronic inflammation of the spinal cord, chronic disease of the kidneys, and commencing cataract of both eyes; the effects of her maladies would be ultimate paralysis of her lower limbs and loss of eyesight. Her condition would never improve considering its nature and her age, they stated.[9] Congress supported the bill without much fuss, increased Mary's pension, and paid her fifteen thousand dollars in back payments.[10]

Mary's mental health also was deteriorating during her final years. She was suffering from a "great mental depression," according to Dr. Sayre, which probably contributed to her preference to rarely leave her room in the Edwards home and remain in the dark, lit only with candles, even during the daytime.[11] Mary accepted visitors, although she did not return visits. Her mania for material possessions had not abated since her time at Bellevue Place. She brought sixty-four trunks of clothing with her to the Edwards home, which she would go through, unpack and repack, for hours every day.[12] Mary had so many trunks in the Edwards's storeroom—weighing about eight thousand pounds—the maid resigned, being afraid to sleep in her quarters under the storeroom for fear the floor would collapse.[13] Mary's niece later remembered her aunt was "a lot of trouble" to the Edwards family, although she was told not to say anything unkind about the widow in her last years "because she wasn't herself."[14]

Mary also continued to have delusions and hallucinations. She would sleep only on one side of her bed to leave "the president's place" on the other side undisturbed, and asked her visitors if they heard her husband's voice.[15] Her biggest fear, however, was for Robert. When she heard

President-elect Garfield had appointed Robert secretary of war, she was terrified. According to one report she would often sit and repeat, "Secretary of war? Secretary of war? Then he'll be shot sure! That's always the way in war!"[16] After Garfield's assassination, it was reported that Mary began suffering "the most intense mental anguish," being so clearly reminded of her husband's murder and becoming frantically afraid that Robert would be murdered as well.[17]

Mary left specific instructions for her funeral, which Robert followed.[18] He attended her funeral and burial in Springfield, and took all of his mother's trunks home to Chicago. Robert's wife, Mary Harlan Lincoln, examined all the clothing and household items, kept what she wanted for herself and the children, and gave the rest to the female members of Robert's family.[19] Robert did not look through the trunks containing the more personal items for ten years.[20] He kept the important family heirlooms, but he did seek to suppress and admit to destroying a number of his mother's letters that she wrote during her "period of mental derangement," as he called it.[21] To his Victorian gentleman's mind, these letters were private family matters not meant for public consumption; of course he also deemed them an embarrassment to the Lincoln legacy.

While Mary Lincoln remained friends with James and Myra Bradwell for years after their assistance in 1875–76—probably for the rest of her life—there is no evidence they attended her funeral. While the Bradwells truly were good friends to Mary Todd Lincoln before and after her commitment to the sanitarium, it was and is their role in her early release that has become their legacy in Mary Lincoln's story. As Mary herself supposedly said, "When all others, among them my husband's supposed friends, failed me in the most bitter hours of my life, these loyal hearts, Myra and James Bradwell, came to my assistance and rescued me under great difficulty from confinement in an insane asylum."[22]

Notes

Bibliography

Index

NOTES

The unpublished manuscript of Myra Pritchard's work, "The Dark Days of Abraham Lincoln's Widow, as Revealed by Her Own Letters," now resides in folder 5, container 8, part 2 of the Robert Todd Lincoln Family Papers in the Manuscripts Division of the Library of Congress. Endnote citations to the manuscript—which may seem like the book is referencing itself—have been made because some of the Mary Lincoln letters Pritchard transcribed exist only in her manuscript. The original letters owned by Pritchard's family for decades, from which her book was written, have not been found.

Pritchard originally divided her manuscript into nine separate sections for serial publication, with each section having its own independent page numbering. Therefore, all citations in this book are by Pritchard's chapter and page number. For example, 2:8 signifies chapter 2, page 8 from the original manuscript.

The following abbreviations have been used to simplify endnote citations:

ALPL	Abraham Lincoln Presidential Library, Springfield, Ill.
CHM	Chicago History Museum, Chicago, Ill.
IF	Mary Todd Lincoln Insanity File, Lincoln Financial Collection, Lincoln Library at Allen County Public Library, Fort Wayne, Ind., courtesy of the State of Indiana.
LB	Robert Todd Lincoln Letterpress Books, Abraham Lincoln Presidential Library, Springfield, Ill. All citations include the volume number, microfilm reel number, and page number of the letter cited. For example, an entry designated as "LB, 1:1:133–39" means vol. 1, reel 1, pages 133–39 in the Letterpress Books.
LOC	Library of Congress, Washington, D.C.
RTLFP	Robert Todd Lincoln Family Papers, Manuscripts Division, Library of Congress.

EDITOR'S INTRODUCTION

1. Myra Pritchard claimed to own thirty-seven letters "written by Mrs. Abraham Lincoln to my grandparents, Judge and Mrs. Bradwell," although she used only thirty-one letters in her book—and not all of them were written by Mary Lincoln. Pritchard stated in chapter 9 that she chose not to publish all the letters in her possession, and her figures indicate that she had six more letters. It appears that Pritchard was a victim of poor semantics in that not all of her thirty-seven letters were written by Mary Lincoln but that she possessed thirty-seven letters *total*, and they were written to and from various people, with the *majority* of them by Mary Lincoln. Also, Pritchard's estate inventory lists a letter from Mary Lincoln to Myra Bradwell dated Aug. 2, 1867, but the manuscript does not include it, and Pritchard herself always said her letters spanned 1872–78. Why this earlier letter was not included is unknown, but it was subsequently discovered by this author in 2008. Myra Helmer Pritchard, "Statement Regarding the Disposal of Mary Lincoln Letters," Mar. 1, 1928, Pritchard Family Papers. A partial list of the letters in Pritchard's possession can be found in the Myra Helmer Pritchard estate inventory, Sept. 19, 1947, Pritchard Family Papers. For the 1867 letter, see Jason Emerson, "New Mary Lincoln Letter Found," *Journal of the Illinois State Historical Society*, 101, nos. 3, 4 (fall-winter 2008): 315–28.
2. Myra Helmer Pritchard, "Statement Regarding the Disposal of Mary Lincoln Letters," Mar. 1, 1928, Myra Pritchard Family Papers.
3. Myra Helmer Pritchard, "The Dark Days of Abraham Lincoln's Widow, as Revealed by Her Own Letters," unpublished manuscript, 2:8, folder 5, cont. 8, part 2, RTLFP. Horner's Lincoln collection was later donated to the Illinois State Historical Library and was the basis for the current collection at the Abraham Lincoln Presidential Library.
4. Eleanor Gridley, affidavit, Mar. 8, 1929, Pritchard Family Papers. Gridley was the author of *The Story of Abraham Lincoln: Or the Journey from the Log Cabin to the White House* (New York: Eaton and Mains, 1900). Lincoln historian Ida M. Tarbell also knew about the letters after James Bradwell mentioned them to her during an interview in the late 1890s. Tarbell did not press Bradwell about the letters, however, as her subject was Abraham Lincoln, not Mary. James Bradwell, interview by Ida Tarbell, n.d., The Ida M. Tarbell–Lincoln Collection, Pelletier Library, Allegheny College, Meadville, Penn.
5. Honoré Willsie Morrow, *Mary Todd Lincoln: An Appreciation of the Wife of Abraham Lincoln* (New York: Morrow, 1928), 6.
6. W. A. Evans, *Mrs. Abraham Lincoln: A Study of Her Personality and Her Influence on Lincoln* (New York: Knopf, 1932), 4.
7. Page 1 of Myra Pritchard's manuscript is stamped "EDITORIAL DEPARTMENT PAID MAY 28, 1927," with a handwritten notation stating, "OK Pay $5,000"; agreement between Myra Pritchard and Liberty Weekly, Inc., Jan. 30, 1928, Pritchard Family Papers. This contract is for the dissolution of the previous publishing contract, dated Apr. 6, 1927. The original contract has not been found.
8. Tarbell's work was the product of extensive original interviews and research, and included previously unpublished Lincoln documents. For the story of her study, see Tarbell's autobiography, *All in the Day's Work* (New York: Macmillan, 1939), 161–79, and Judith A. Rice, "Ida M. Tarbell: A Progressive Look at Lincoln," *Journal of the*

Abraham Lincoln Association 19, no. 1 (winter 1998): 57–72. Her resulting book was *The Life of Abraham Lincoln*, 2 vols. (New York: McClure, Phillips, 1900). Tarbell also wrote *Father Abraham* (1909) and *In the Footsteps of the Lincolns* (1924).

9. Frederic Towers to Katherine Helm, Oct. 14, 1927, 1928.32, Lincoln Collection, Friends of Hildene, Inc., Manchester, Vt., also in folder "Correspondence 1896, 1926–1927," F box 3, William H. Townsend Collection, 1998 MS 005, Special Collections and Digital Programs, University of Kentucky Libraries, Margaret I. King Library, University of Kentucky.
10. Frederic Towers to Myra Pritchard, Oct. 14, 1927, 1928.32.1, Lincoln Collection, Friends of Hildene, Inc., Manchester, Vt.
11. Robert Lincoln to Abram Wakeman, Nov. 28, 1908, LB, 41:71:430; Robert Lincoln to Le Grand Van Valkenburgh, May 26, 1913, Robert Todd Lincoln Papers, Lincoln Collection, ALPL; Robert Lincoln to Emily Todd Helm, June 15, 1913, Robert Todd Lincoln Papers, CHM.
12. Myra Helmer Pritchard, "Statement regarding the Disposal of Mary Lincoln Letters," Mar. 1, 1928, Pritchard Family Papers.
13. The records do not indicate to which three letters they objected. The letters from Mary Lincoln to Myra Bradwell dated June 18, July 7, and July 14, 1876, seem most plausible due not only to their rancorous content but also to the private nature of the property issues involved.
14. Frederic Towers to Otis Rockwood, Dec. 28, 1927, folder 4, cont. 8, part 2, RTLFP.
15. The case involved Mrs. Woodrow Wilson and Col. Edward M. House. House wanted to publish some of President Wilson's letters to him, but Mrs. Wilson refused. Edward M. House diary, Nov. 22, 1925, entry, Edward M. House Papers, Yale University Library, cited in Godfrey Hodgen, *Woodrow Wilson's Right Hand: The Life of Col. Edward M. House* (New Haven: Yale University Press, 2006), 260–61, 310 n. 13.
16. Frederic Towers to Otis Rockwood, Dec. 28, 1927, folder 4, cont. 8, part 2, RTLFP.
17. Otis Rockwood to Frederic Towers, Jan. 6, 1928, folder 4, cont. 8, part 2, RTLFP.
18. Frederic Towers to N. Otis Rockwood, Jan. 17, 1928, and N. Otis Rockwood to Frederic Towers, Jan. 19, 1928, and Bert C. Farrar to Frederic Towers, Washington, D.C., Feb. 1, 1928, folder 4, cont. 8, part 2, RTLFP; Frederic Towers to Katherine Helm, Jan. 27, 1928, folder "K Helm Correspondence 1928–1930," F box 2, William H. Townsend Collection, 1998 MS 005, Special Collections and Digital Programs, University of Kentucky Libraries, Margaret I. King Library, University of Kentucky.
19. Signed agreement between Myra Pritchard, Norman B. Frost, and Frederic N. Towers, Jan. 31, 1928, folder 4, cont. 8, part 2, RTLFP, and Pritchard Family Papers.
20. Karl Harriman to Whitney Payne, Mar. 21, 1929, Pritchard Family Papers.
21. Agreement between Myra Pritchard and Liberty Weekly, Inc., Jan. 30, 1928, Pritchard Family Papers.
22. W. R. Dillon, "Memo: re Myra Pritchard Estate Lincoln Collection," Sept. 11, 1947, p. 4, Pritchard Family Papers.
23. W. A. Evans wanted to see the letters to include in his book *Mrs. Abraham Lincoln: A Study of Her Personality and Her Influence on Abraham Lincoln*, which he was in the midst of writing. Ella McCaleb was a friend of Myra Pritchard and fellow alumna from Vassar College, who had seen the letters. She mentioned them to William Adams Slade, chief of bibliography at the Library of Congress (who was "married to a Vassar woman"), and he asked if there was any way the library could acquire

them. W. A. Evans, M.D., to Myra Pritchard, Nov. 24, 1928, and Ella McCaleb to Myra Pritchard, Nov. 21, 1928, folder 4, cont. 8, part 2, RTLFP.

24. Myra Pritchard to Frederic Towers, Nov. 28, 1928, and Frederic Towers to Myra Pritchard, Dec. 4, 1928, folder 4, cont. 8, part 2, RTLFP.
25. Henry Horner to Myra Pritchard, Mar. 4, 1929, and Myra Pritchard to Henry Horner, Mar. 14, 1929, personal correspondence folder, Pi-Q, box 7, Henry Horner Lincoln Collection Papers, Manuscripts Division, ALPL. Sandburg in fact makes no mention of the Bradwells, Myra Pritchard, or the Bradwell-Lincoln correspondence in his 1932 book, *Mary Lincoln, Wife and Widow.*
26. Agreement between Myra Pritchard and the Trustees of the Chicago Historical Society, Oct. 22, 1932, and Myra Pritchard to L. H. Shattuck, Oct. 23, 1932, Mrs. Myra (Stuart) Pritchard File, CHM; Myra Pritchard to the president of the Trustees of the Chicago Historical Society, Battle Creek, Mich., Oct. 22, 1932, and Eleanor Gridley, affidavit, Mar. 8, 1929, Pritchard Family Papers.
27. Margreta Pritchard, "Affidavit re Destruction of Liberty Magazine Manuscript Relative to Mary Lincoln Letters," Sept. 18, 1947, Pritchard Family Papers.
28. "Mrs. Lincoln, Widow of President's Son: Married Emancipator's Only Son in Washington in 1868—Dies in Capitol at 90," *New York Times*, Apr. 1, 1937, clipping in Lincoln Family Folder, box 15, Randall Family Papers, Manuscripts Department, Library of Congress.
29. W. R. Dillon, "Memo: re Myra Pritchard Estate Lincoln Collection," Sept. 11, 1947, p. 5, Pritchard Family Papers.
30. L. Thorne Arthur to Margreta Pritchard, Sept. 12, 1947, and Affidavit re: Destruction of Copies of Mary Lincoln Collection, signed by Margreta Pritchard, Mar. 19, 1951, Pritchard Family Papers.
31. Ella McCaleb to Myra Pritchard, Nov. 21, 1928, and W. A. Evans to Myra Pritchard, Chicago, Nov. 24, 1928, folder 4, cont. 8, part 2, RTLFP; Henrietta Horner to Ruth Painter Randall, Sept. 26, 1949, cont. 65, Randall Family Papers, Manuscripts Division, Library of Congress; Ruth Painter Randall, *Mary Lincoln: Biography of a Marriage* (Boston: Little, Brown, 1953), 434.
32. For full story of the discovery see Jason Emerson, *The Madness of Mary Lincoln* (Carbondale: Southern Illinois University Press, 2007), 140–50.
33. Pritchard's manuscript was never copyrighted, which makes it public domain. Even if it were not, the last descendant of the Pritchard family, the owners of the manuscript, and the Abraham Lincoln Presidential Library (which was given ownership and copyright over all Lincoln-related items by Robert Todd Lincoln Beckwith) all waived any objection to publication. The manuscript is now in the manuscript collections of the Library of Congress, where it also is listed as having no copyright restrictions.

CHAPTER 1

1. "Deed of Gift of Manuscripts and Private Papers of President Lincoln by His Son, Robert Todd Lincoln," Jan. 23, 1923, and St. George L. Sioussat to David C. Mearns, internal Library of Congress memorandum, Apr. 1, 1947, and David C. Mearns to the Librarian of Congress, "Property Rights, Lincoln Manuscripts and the Seward Heirs," July 17, 1951, David C. Mearns Papers, Manuscripts Division, Library of Congress; Robert Lincoln deed of gift to Library of Congress, Jan. 23, 1923, part 2,

cont. 2, RTLFP; David C. Mearns, *The Lincoln Papers: The Story of the Collection with Selections to July 4, 1861*, 2 vols. (Garden City, N.Y.: Doubleday, 1948), 1:111–36.

2. Mearns, *Lincoln Papers*, 1:134; Robert Lincoln to Albert J. Beveridge, Washington, Jan. 23, 1923, folder "L," box 290, Albert J. Beveridge Papers, Manuscripts Division, Library of Congress.
3. Myra Helmer Pritchard, "Statement regarding the Disposal of Mary Lincoln Letters," Mar. 1, 1928, Myra Pritchard Family Papers, privately owned.
4. See "Clouded Reason: Trial of Mrs. Abraham Lincoln for Insanity," *Chicago Tribune*, May 20, 1875, 1; "Mrs. Lincoln: The Widow of the Martyred President Adjudged Insane in County Court," *Chicago Inter Ocean*, May 20, 1875, 1; "A Sad Revelation: Mrs. Mary Lincoln, the Widow of the Late President, Adjudged Insane," *Chicago Times*, Thursday, May 20, 1875, 2. The details of the trial will be discussed in later chapters. For a full examination of the trial see also Jason Emerson, *The Madness of Mary Lincoln* (Carbondale: Southern Illinois University Press, 2007), 44–62.
5. Myra Helmer Pritchard, "Statement regarding the Disposal of Mary Lincoln Letters," Mar. 1, 1928, Pritchard Family Papers.
6. "Agreement between Myra Helmer Pritchard and Liberty Weekly," Jan. 30, 1928, Pritchard Family Papers.
7. *Myra Bradwell v. State of Illinois*, 83 U.S. 130 (1872); Jane M. Friedman, *America's First Woman Lawyer* (Buffalo, N.Y.: Prometheus Books, 1993), 18; Nancy T. Gilliam, "A Professional Pioneer: Myra Bradwell's Fight to Practice Law," *Law and History Review*, 5:1 (spring 1987): 105–13; James Bradwell, interview by Ida Tarbell, n.d., Ida M. Tarbell–Lincoln Collection, Pelletier Library, Allegheny College, Meadville, Penn.; "Pioneer Lawyer at Death's Door," *Chicago Tribune*, Nov. 29, 1907, 5.
8. Lelia J. Robinson, "Women Lawyers in the United States," *Green Bag* 2, no. 1 (Jan. 1890): 14; "Bessie Bradwell Helmer," *Woman's Who's Who in America* (New York: American Commonwealth, 1914), 379; "Frank A. Helmer," *Chicago Law Times*, Catherine V. Waite, ed., vol. 2 (Chicago: Waite, 1888), 378–80.
9. "Lincoln Pen Brings $2,300 at Auction Sale," n.d., clipping in Robert Todd Lincoln Papers, ALPL; "Lincoln's Emancipation Pen Disputed; Woman in West Protests Sale of One Here," *New York Times*, Feb. 26, 1929, and "Tooth Marked Pen of Lincoln Shown in City," n.d., clippings in Pritchard Family Papers.
10. Myra Pritchard to directors of the Chicago Historical Society, Battle Creek, Mich., Oct. 16, 1932, and agreement between Myra Pritchard and the Trustees of the Chicago Historical Society, Oct. 22, 1932, Mrs. Myra (Stuart) Pritchard File, Manuscripts Division, CHM; Eleanor Gridley, affidavit, Mar. 8, 1929, and L. Thorne Arthur to Margreta Pritchard, Sept. 12, 1947, and W. R. Dillon, "Memorandum Re: Myra Pritchard Estate Lincoln Collection," Sept. 11, 1947, Pritchard Family Papers; Carl Sandburg, *The Lincoln Collector: The Story of the Oliver R. Barrett Lincoln Collection* (New York: Bonanza Books, 1960), 195.
11. "Definition of Democracy," Aug. 1, 1858 [?], in Roy P. Basler, ed., Marion Dolores Pratt and Lloyd A. Dunlap, asst. eds., *The Collected Works of Abraham Lincoln*, 9 vols. (New Brunswick, N.J.: Rutgers University Press, 1953–55), 2:532; James Bradwell interview, "Lincoln's Definition of Democracy," *Chicago Times-Herald*, reprinted in *New York Times*, Sept. 13, 1895, 10.
12. William H. Herndon and Jesse W. Weik, *Herndon's Lincoln*, Douglas L. Wilson and Rodney O. Davis, eds. (1889; repr., Urbana: University of Illinois Press, 2006), 264–65n.

13. For excellent studies of the William Herndon–Mary Lincoln relationship see David Donald, "Herndon and Mrs. Lincoln," in *Lincoln Reconsidered* (New York: Alfred A. Knopf, 1956), 37–56, and Douglas L. Wilson, "William H. Herndon and Mary Todd Lincoln," *Journal of the Abraham Lincoln Association* 22 (summer 2001): 1–26. For the best study of Herndon's personality see David Donald, *Lincoln's Herndon* (New York: Alfred A. Knopf, 1948). For Herndon's philosophy of history, especially about Abraham and Mary Lincoln as his subjects, see his letters in Emanuel Hertz, *The Hidden Lincoln: From the Letters and Papers of William H. Herndon* (New York: Viking, 1938).
14. See James S. Brust, "The Psychiatric Illness of Mary Lincoln," in Emerson, *The Madness of Mary Lincoln*, 185–90; Jennifer L. Bach, "Was Mary Todd Lincoln Bipolar?" *Journal of Illinois History* 8, no. 4 (winter 2005): 281–94. For other professional medical opinions of Mary Lincoln, see W. A. Evans, *Mrs. Abraham Lincoln: A Study of Her Personality and Her Influence on Abraham Lincoln* (New York: Knopf, 1932); James A. Brussel, "Mary Todd Lincoln: A Psychiatric Study," *Psychiatric Quarterly* 15, supp. 1 (Jan. 1941): 7–26; John M. Suarez, "Mary Todd Lincoln: A Case Study," *American Journal of Psychiatry* 122, no. 7 (Jan. 1966): 816–19; Norbert Hirschhorn and Robert G. Feldman, "Mary Lincoln's Final Illness: A Medical and Historical Reappraisal," *Journal of the History of Medicine and Allied Sciences* 54, no. 4 (Oct. 1999): 511–42; Deborah Hayden, *Pox: Genius, Madness, and the Mysteries of Syphilis* (New York: Basic Books, 2003), 120–32.
15. Elizabeth Edwards, interview with William Herndon, January 10, 1866, 2:220–226, LN 2408, Ward Hill Lamon Papers, Huntington Library; Herndon and Weik, *Herndon's Life of Lincoln*, 135; James C. Conkling to Mercy Ann Levering, September 21, 1840, folder 1, box 1, Conkling Family Papers, ALPL; Ninian Edwards quoted in Katherine Helm, *The True Story of Mary, Wife of Lincoln* (New York: Harper, 1928), 81.
16. Herndon and Weik, *Herndon's Lincoln*, 137. See also Elizabeth Todd Edwards interview by William Herndon, 1865–66, and Elizabeth and Ninian Edwards interview by Jesse Weik, in Douglas L. Wilson and Rodney O. Davis, eds., *Herndon's Informants: Letters, Interviews, and Statements about Abraham Lincoln* (Urbana: University of Illinois Press, 1998), 443, 592; Douglas L. Wilson, "Abraham Lincoln and 'That Fatal First of January,'" *Civil War History*, 38, no. 2 (June 1992): 101–30; Douglas L. Wilson, *Honor's Voice: The Transformation of Abraham Lincoln* (New York: Knopf, 1998), 221–31; Ida M. Tarbell, *The Life of Abraham Lincoln* (New York: Lincoln Memorial Association, 1900), 1:172–79.
17. Tarbell, *Life of Abraham Lincoln*, 176–79.
18. William E. Barton, *The Life of Abraham Lincoln*, 2 vols. (New York: Bobbs-Merrill, 1925), 1:260–61.
19. For one of the best descriptions of Lincoln's duel, see Douglas L. Wilson, *Honor's Voice: The Transformation of Abraham Lincoln* (New York: Knopf, 1998), 265–92. See also Roy P. Basler, "The Authorship of the 'Rebecca' Letters," *Abraham Lincoln Quarterly* 2, no. 2 (June 1942): 80–90.
20. Herndon and Weik, *Herndon's Lincoln*, 144n.
21. See James H. Matheny to William Herndon, Springfield, Ill., Aug. 21, 1888, Wilson and Davis, *Herndon's Informants*, 665–66.
22. Jean H. Baker, *Mary Todd Lincoln: A Biography* (New York: Norton, 1987), 120.
23. Mary Lincoln to Alexander Williamson, Chicago, Aug. 19, 1866, Justin G. Turner and Linda Levitt Turner, *Mary Todd Lincoln: Her Life and Letters* (New York: Knopf,

1972), 382; Mary Lincoln to Elizabeth Swing, Mar. 12, 1874, Lincoln Collection, ALPL, printed in Thomas F. Schwartz, "'My stay on Earth, is growing very short,' Mary Todd Lincoln's Letters to Willis Danforth and Elizabeth Swing," *Journal of Illinois History* 6 (summer 2003): 129.

24. Emphasis in original. Mary Lincoln to Elizabeth Keckley, Oct. 29, 1867, Turner and Turner, *Mary Todd Lincoln*, 447.

25. This statement often has been taken to mean Mary was an adulterer, but the context of the debate clearly shows Yates was accusing her of being a Confederate sympathizer. F. Lauristan Bullard, "Mrs. Lincoln's Pension," *Lincoln Herald*, vol. 49 (1947): 25. See also Mark E. Neely, "Abraham Lincoln did NOT Defend His Wife before the Committee on the Conduct of the War," *Lincoln Lore*, no. 1643, Jan. 1975, and Neely, "Thurlow Weed, The New York Custom House, and Mrs. Lincoln's 'Treason,'" *Lincoln Lore*, no. 1679, Jan. 1978.

26. Elizabeth Keckley, *Behind the Scenes, or Thirty Years a Slave and Four Years in the White House* (1868; repr., New York: Arno Press, 1968), 135–36.

27. William O. Stoddard, *Inside the White House in War Times*, Michael Burlingame, ed. (1891; repr., Lincoln: University of Nebraska Press, 2000), 32, 48, 182; Julia Taft Bayne, *Tad Lincoln's Father* (1931; repr., Lincoln: University of Nebraska Press, 2001), 72; Anna L. Boyden, *War Reminiscences, or Echoes from Hospital and White House* (Boston: Lathrop, 1887), 60, 119–20; Louis A. Warren, "Mrs. Lincoln and 'Your Soldier Boy,'" *Lincoln Lore*, no. 683, May 11, 1942; Ruth Painter Randall, *Mary Lincoln: Biography of a Marriage* (Boston: Little, Brown, 1953), 231–41.

28. Keckley, *Behind the Scenes*, 104–5, 181–82. See also Boyden, *War Reminiscences*, 51–59.

29. Katherine Helm, *The True Story of Mary, Wife of Lincoln* (New York: Harper, 1928), 225–26.

30. "Mrs. Lincoln's Wardrobe," *Chicago Tribune*, Oct. 8, 1867, 2; "Mrs. Lincoln," *Illinois Daily State Journal*, October 10, 1867, 1; "Mrs. Lincoln's Wardrobe," *The Independent*, Oct. 17, 1867, 4; "The Widow of Lincoln," *The Round Table: A Saturday Review of Politics, Finance, Literature, Society*, Oct. 12, 1867, 240; Keckley, *Behind the Scenes*, 267–331; Davis to Miss Addie Burr, July 19, 1882, Adeline Ellery (Burr) Davis Green Papers, Rare Book, Manuscript, and Special Collections Library, Duke University, Durham, North Carolina. For Robert Lincoln's reaction, see Mary Todd Lincoln to Elizabeth Keckley, Oct. 6, 1867, Turner and Turner, *Mary Todd Lincoln*, 440, and Robert T. Lincoln to Mary Harlan, Oct. 16, 1867, quoted in Helm, *True Story of Mary*, 267–77.

31. *Congressional Globe*, 40th Congress, 3rd sess., 1869, 2:1242–45 and 41st Cong., 2nd sess., 1870, 5:4540–41 and 6:5559–60; F. Lauriston Bullard, "Mrs. Lincoln's Pension," *Lincoln Herald* 49, no. 2 (June 1947): 22–27. For Mary's letters on the issue, see Turner and Turner, *Mary Todd Lincoln*, 491–589.

32. "Obituary: Death of Thomas Lincoln, Youngest Son of the Late President," *Chicago Tribune*, July 16, 1871, 3; "Death of Tad Lincoln," *New York Times*, July 16, 1871, 1; John Hay, "Tad Lincoln," *Chicago Tribune*, July 19, 1871, 1; Milton H. Shutes, "Mortality of the Five Lincoln Boys," *Lincoln Herald* 57, nos. 1–2 (spring-summer 1955): 7; W. A. Evans, *Mrs. Abraham Lincoln: A Study of Her Personality and Her Influence on Lincoln* (New York: Knopf, 1932), 340. For an excellent and exhaustive medical survey of Tad's final illness and death, see John G. Sotos, *The Physical Lincoln Sourcebook*, printing 1.1a (Mt Vernon, Va.: Mt. Vernon Book Systems, 2008), 344–49, ¶¶5264–5329.

33. Emphasis in original. Mary Lincoln to Myra Bradwell, Nov. 1, 1872, photographic copy, folder 1, cont. 8, part 2, RTLFP.
34. Mary Lincoln to Elizabeth Emerson Atwater, Racine, June 30, 1867, Turner and Turner, *Mary Todd Lincoln*, 425; F. Lauristan Bullard, *Tad and His Father* (Boston: Little, Brown, 1917), 2.
35. Mary Lincoln to Elizabeth Keckley, Oct. 6, 1867, and to David Davis, Nov. 9, 1871, Turner and Turner, *Mary Todd Lincoln*, 440, 597; "Obituary: Death of Thomas Lincoln," *Chicago Tribune*, July 16, 1871, 3.

CHAPTER 2

1. Emphasis in original. Mary Lincoln to Mary Jane Welles, Chicago, Dec. 29, 1865, Turner and Turner, *Mary Todd Lincoln*, 315.
2. Robert T. Lincoln to Mary Harlan, Oct. 16, 1867, quoted in Helm, *True Story of Mary*, 267–77; Mary Lincoln to Mary Harlan Lincoln, London, Nov. 22, 1870, folder 1, box 1, and Elizabeth Edwards to Robert Lincoln, Nov. 12, 1875, folder 16, box 2, IF; Francis B. Carpenter, interview by *Boston Globe*, "Met at a Dance: Romantic Story of President Lincoln's Courtship," *Boston Globe*, Feb. 17, 1895, 31.
3. Evans, *Mrs. Abraham Lincoln*, 342; Hirschhorn and Feldman, "Mary Lincoln's Final Illness," 536; Sotos, *Physical Lincoln Sourcebook*, 269–78, 281–85.
4. Jane Grey Swisshelm, *Half a Century* (Chicago: Jansen, McClurg, 1880), 236–37.
5. Mary Lincoln to Myra Bradwell, Jan. 26, 1873, Pritchard, "Dark Days," 2:2.
6. Mary Lincoln to Jacob Bunn, Pau, France, Jan. 31, 1877, Turner and Turner, *Mary Todd Lincoln*, 623–24; Mary Lincoln to James Bradwell, Oct. 10, 1872, folder 2, box 1, IF.
7. Mary Lincoln to Willis Danforth, n.d., in Thomas F. Schwartz, "'My stay on Earth is growing very short': Mary Todd Lincoln's Letters to Willis Danforth and Elizabeth Swing," *Journal of Illinois History* 6 (summer 2003): 135; Elizabeth Edwards to Robert Lincoln, Springfield, Nov. 5, 1875, folder 16, box 2, IF; testimony of Mrs. Allen, "Clouded Reason," *Chicago Tribune*, May 20, 1875, 1.
8. Emphasis in original. Mary Lincoln to Myra Bradwell, May 6, 1874, Pritchard, "Dark Days," 2:3–4.
9. Eddie Foy and Alvin F. Harlow, "Clowning through Life," *Collier's Weekly* (Dec. 25, 1926): 15–16, 30.
10. Emphasis in original. Mary Lincoln to Myra Bradwell, Feb. 20, 1875, photographic copies of first and last pages in folder 1, cont. 8, part 2, RTLFP, full letter in Pritchard, "Dark Days," 2:4–7.
11. Edwards to Bradwell, Aug. 3, 1875, copy in Myra Bradwell's handwriting on *Chicago Legal News* stationery, folder 1, cont. 8, part 2, RTLFP; Elizabeth Edwards to Robert Lincoln, Aug. 12, 1875, folder 16, box 2, IF.
12. Barton, *Life of Abraham Lincoln*, 2:418–19.
13. Paul Angle to Henry Horner, Sept. 25 and Oct. 1, 1925, folder "1925 D-H," box 2, Abraham Lincoln Association Papers, Manuscripts Division, ALPL; William E. Barton, prefatory note, Feb. 12, 1926, William E. Barton Scrapbook, vol. 47, "The Insanity of Mary Lincoln," Lincoln Collection, Department of Special Collections, University of Chicago Library; Barton, *Life of Abraham Lincoln*, 2:418–19; William E. Barton, *The Women Lincoln Loved* (Indianapolis: Bobbs-Merrill, 1927), 362. See also Mark E. Neely and R. Gerald McMurtry, *The Insanity File: The Case of Mary Todd Lincoln* (Carbondale: Southern Illinois University Press, 1986), 123–24.
14. All four documents are in folder 33, box 2, IF, and in vol. 47, Barton Scrapbook.

15. Ibid.
16. For full backgrounds on all seven physicians, see Emerson, *Madness of Mary Lincoln*, 50–51.
17. Barton, *Life of Abraham Lincoln*, 2:418–19.
18. "Clouded Reason: Trial of Mrs. Abraham Lincoln for Insanity," *Chicago Tribune*, May 20, 1875, 1.
19. Statement of Dr. Ralph N. Isham, May 18, 1875, Cook County Court Documents, folder 33, box 2, IF.
20. Mary Lincoln to Edward Isham, two telegrams, Jacksonville, Fla., Mar. 12, 1875, and J. J. S. Wilson, supt., to station manager, telegram, Jacksonville, Fla., undated, and John Coyne, manager, to J. J. S. Wilson, for Robert T. Lincoln, telegram, Jacksonville, Fla., Mar. 12, 1875, and John Coyne, manager, to J. S. S. Wilson, supt., telegram, Jacksonville, Fla., Mar. 13 1875, and Mary Lincoln to Robert Lincoln, telegram, Jacksonville, Fla., Mar. 13, 1875, folder 3, box 1, IF; "Clouded Reason," *Chicago Tribune*, May 20, 1875, 1; "Mrs. Lincoln: The Widow of the Martyred President Adjudged Insane in County Court," *Chicago Inter Ocean*, May 20, 1875, 1; "A Sad Revelation: Mrs. Mary Lincoln, the Widow of the Late President, Adjudged Insane," *Chicago Times*, May 20, 1875, 2.
21. "Clouded Reason," *Chicago Tribune*, May 20, 1875, 1.
21. "Clouded Reason" *Chicago Tribune*, May 20, 1875, 1; "Mrs. Lincoln," *Chicago Inter Ocean*, May 20, 1875, 1; Leonard Swett to David Davis, Chicago, May 24, 1875, folder A-73, box 5, Davis Family Papers; "A Sad Revelation," *Chicago Times*, May 20, 1875, 2.
23. "Clouded Reason" *Chicago Tribune*, May 20, 1875, 1; "Mrs. Lincoln," *Chicago Inter Ocean*, May 20, 1875, 1.
24. For his description of his experience on the day of Mary Lincoln's insanity trial, see Leonard Swett to David Davis, Chicago, May 24, 1875, folder A-73, box 5, David Davis Family Papers, ALPL.
25. Lyman J. Gage to William E. Barton, Point Loma, California, Jan. 20, 1921, vol. 47, Barton Scrapbook; Verdict of Jury Declaring Mary Lincoln Insane, May 19, 1875, Cook County Court Documents, folder 33, box 2, IF.
26. Leonard Swett gave a detailed account of Mary's suicide attempt in Swett to David Davis, Chicago, May 24, 1875, folder A-73, box 5, David Davis Family Papers. See also Norbert Hirschhorn, "Mary Lincoln's 'Suicide Attempt': A Physician Reconsiders the Evidence," *Lincoln Herald* 104, no. 3 (fall 2003): 94–98.
27. Leonard Swett to David Davis, Chicago, May 24, 1875, folder A-73, box 5, Davis Family Papers; "A Mind Diseased: The Evidence of Mrs. Lincoln's Mental Aberration," *Illinois State Journal*, May 29, 1875, 2; "Insanity's Freaks," *Chicago Times*, May 21, 1875, clipping in folder 31, box 2, IF.
28. Appointment of Robert T. Lincoln as Conservator for Estate of Mary Lincoln, June 14, 1875, Cook County Court Documents, folder 33, box 2, IF; photostats in pp. 13–16, vol. 47, Barton Scrapbook.
29. Inventory of Real and Personal Estate of Mary Lincoln, May 19, 1875, folder 33, box 2, IF; photostats in p. 18–22, vol. 47, Barton Scrapbook.

CHAPTER 3

1. Deed Record H, 310–11, Manuscripts Division, Illinois Regional Archives Depository, University of Illinois at Springfield; Mary Lincoln to Eliza Stuart Steele, Chicago, May 23, 1871, Turner and Turner, *Mary Todd Lincoln*, 588.

2. James T. Hickey, "The Lincolns' Globe Tavern: A Study in Tracing the History of a Nineteenth Century Building," *Collected Writings*, 59; Frances Todd Wallace, interview by William Herndon, 1865–66, Wilson and Davis, *Herndon's Informants*, 485.
3. Quoted from Honoré Willsie Morrow, *Mary Todd Lincoln: An Appreciation of the Wife of Abraham Lincoln* (New York: William Morrow, 1928), 84. Morrow does not cite her source for this quote.
4. Turner and Turner, *Mary Todd Lincoln*, 247; Jean H. Baker, *Mary Todd Lincoln: A Biography* (New York: W. W. Norton, 1987), 258; Keckley, *Behind the Scenes*, 204; see also Willard L. King, *Lincoln's Manager: David Davis* (Cambridge: Harvard University Press, 1960), 235–37. For a complete explanation of the administration of Abraham Lincoln's estate, see Harry E. Pratt, *The Personal Finances of Abraham Lincoln* (Springfield: Abraham Lincoln Association, 1943), 131–41.
5. Robert T. Lincoln to Mary Harlan, Oct. 16, 1867, quoted in Helm, *True Story of Mary*, 267–77; Mary Lincoln to Alexander Williamson, Chicago, Aug. 17, 1865, and to Sally Orne, Chicago, Dec. 30, 1865, Turner and Turner, *Mary Todd Lincoln*, 264–65, 318–19.
6. The Bellevue Place patient records are privately owned, but a transcript of entries relating to Mary Lincoln was printed by Rodney A. Ross, "Mary Todd Lincoln: Patient at Bellevue Place, Batavia." *Journal of the Illinois State Historical Society* 63, no. 1 (spring 1970): 5–34.
7. Noah Brooks, *Washington in Lincoln's Time*, ed. Herbert Mitgang (New York: Rinehart, 1958).
8. "A Double Crime: Robbery and Murder," *Illinois State Register*, April 29, 1871; *History of Sangamon County, Illinois* (Chicago: Interstate Publishing, 1881), 528–29.
9. Emphasis added. "Mrs. Lincoln: A Visit to Her by 'The Post and Mail' Correspondent: How She Passes the Time at Dr. Patterson's Retreat," *Chicago Post and Mail*, July 13, 1875. Parts of the *Post and Mail* article also were reprinted in Roberta Campbell, "Reporter Visits with Mrs. Lincoln," *Batavia Herald*, Feb. 9, 1983, clipping in Batavia Historical Society, Batavia, Ill.
10. "Patient Progress Reports for Bellevue Place," 48, transcribed in Ross, "Mary Todd Lincoln," 31.
11. "Mrs. Lincoln: A Visit to Her by 'The Post and Mail' Correspondent: How She Passes the Time at Dr. Patterson's Retreat," *Chicago Post and Mail*, July 13, 1875, clipping, Pritchard Family Papers; Bellevue Place Sanitarium advertising brochures, n.d., 2 pages, and 1895, 15 pages, Batavia Historical Society, Batavia, Illinois.
12. "Mrs. Lincoln," *Chicago Post and Mail*, July 13, 1875; Robert Lincoln to Elizabeth Edwards, Aug. 7, 1875, LB, 1:1:133–39. See also *Past and Present of Kane County, Illinois* (Chicago: W. Le Baron Jr. & Co., 1878), 296–311.
13. "Mrs. Lincoln: Is the Widow of President Lincoln a Prisoner?" *Chicago Morning Courier*, Sept. 4, 1875, clipping, Pritchard Family Papers.
14. Argus Eye, letter to the editor, n.p., Sept. 4, 1875, and "Mrs. Lincoln's Friends Not Allowed to See Her," n.p., Sept. 4, 1875, clippings, Pritchard Family Papers.
15. Mary Lincoln to James Bradwell, July 28, 1875, photographic copy, folder 1, cont. 8, part 2, RTLFP.
16. James Bradwell to John Todd Stuart, Chicago, July 30, 1875, Pritchard, "Dark Days," 3:12.
17. Stephen Berry, *House of Abraham: Lincoln and the Todds, a Family Divided by War* (Boston: Houghton Mifflin, 2007), 132–36; Doris Replogle Porter, "The Mysterious Browning Letter," *Lincoln Herald* 90, no. 1 (spring 1988): 20–23.

18. Emphasis in original. Myra Bradwell to Elizabeth Edwards, July 30, 1875, Pritchard, "Dark Days," 3:13.
19. Elizabeth Edwards to Robert Lincoln, Springfield, Aug. 11, 1875, folder 16, box 2, IF.
20. Emphasis in original. Elizabeth Edwards to Myra Bradwell, Aug. 3, 1875, copy in Myra Bradwell's handwriting on *Chicago Legal News* stationery, folder 1, cont. 8, part 2, RTLFP.
21. John Todd Stuart to Robert Lincoln, May 10 and May 21, 1875, and to Leonard Swett, May 21, 1875, folder 26, box 2, IF; Elizabeth Edwards to Robert Lincoln, Springfield, Aug. 12, 1875, and Oct. 29, 1876, folder 16, box 2, IF; "Mrs. Lincoln," *Illinois State Journal*, Oct. 10, 1867, 1, "Patient Progress Reports for Bellevue Place," 47, 51, transcribed in Ross, "Mary Todd Lincoln," 31, 32; Robert Lincoln to Elizabeth Edwards, Aug. 10, 1875, LB, 1:1:141–42.

CHAPTER 4

1. Mary Lincoln to Francis B. Carpenter, Nov. 15, 1865, Turner and Turner, *Mary Todd Lincoln*, 284–85; Mary Lincoln, interview by William Herndon, Sept. 1866, 2:227–28, LN 2408, Ward Hill Lamon Papers, Manuscripts Department, Huntington Library, San Marino, Calif., also in Wilson and Davis, *Herndon's Informants*, 359; John Todd Stuart, interview with John G. Nicolay, June 24, 1875, Michael Burlingame, ed., *An Oral History of Abraham Lincoln: John G. Nicolay's Interviews and Essays* (Carbondale: Southern Illinois University Press, 1996), 14; Herndon and Weik, *Herndon's Lincoln*, 290.
2. Robert Lincoln to Mrs. James H. (Sally) Orne, June 1, 1875, folder 2, Robert Todd Lincoln papers, CHM, this letter is also printed in full in Helm, *True Story of Mary*, 295–96; Robert Lincoln to John Hay, June 6, 1875, microfilm reel 8, John Milton Hay Collection, John Hay Library, Brown University, Providence, R.I.; Ross, "Mary Todd Lincoln Patient at Bellevue Place," 11.
3. Robert Lincoln to Mary Harlan Lincoln, July 15, 1871, quoted in Helm, *True Story of Mary*, 294.
4. Emphasis in original. Mary Lincoln to Myra Bradwell, Aug. 3, 1875, Pritchard, "Dark Days," 4:2–4.
5. Robert Lincoln to Henry T. Blow, date illegible (probably between Aug. 3 and Aug. 7), LB, 1:1:127–31.
6. Emphasis in original. Mary Lincoln to Myra Bradwell, n.d., 1875, Pritchard, "Dark Days," 4:4–5. This letter was probably written on the same day as the previous letter, Aug. 3, judging from its placement in Pritchard's chronological manuscript, the mention in the Bellevue Place daily patient progress reports about Mary receiving a letter from Myra Bradwell on August 1, and its reference to the black alpaca materials from the previous letter.
7. Emphasis in original. Robert Lincoln to Elizabeth Edwards, Aug. 10, 1875, LB, 1:1:141–42; "Mrs. Lincoln: A Visit to Her by 'The Post and Mail' Correspondent," *Chicago Post and Mail*, July 13, 1875; "Mrs. Lincoln," *Illinois State Journal*, May 24, 1875. For an interesting reminiscence of Mary Lincoln shopping in the nearby town of Aurora while a patient at Bellevue Place, see Lutz White, "Now and Then: Before the Tardy Bell Rings," *Aurora (Ill.) Beacon-News*, Dec. 18, 1932, 6.
8. Mary Lincoln to James Bradwell, Aug. 8, 1875, photographic copy, folder 1, cont. 8, part 2, RTLFP.
9. Mary Lincoln to Adeline Judd, June 13, 1860, and Mary Lincoln to Elizabeth Todd Grimsley, Sept. 28, 1861, Turner and Turner, *Mary Todd Lincoln*, 64, 105.

10. Emphasis in original. Mary Lincoln to Myra Bradwell, Friday, Aug. 1875, photographic copy of one page of letter and copy of first half of letter in Myra Bradwell's handwriting on *Chicago Legal News* stationery in folder 1, cont. 8, part 2, RTLFP; complete letter in Pritchard, "Dark Days," 4:7–8. Judging from Pritchard's placement of the letter in her manuscript as well as its contents, this seems to have been written around Aug. 8, 1875.
11. "Patient Progress Reports for Bellevue Place," p. 51, transcribed in Ross, "Mary Todd Lincoln, Patient at Bellevue Place," 32; Robert Lincoln to Elizabeth Edwards, Aug. 7, 1875, LB, 1:1:133–34.
12. Robert Lincoln to Elizabeth Edwards, Aug. 7, 1875, LB, 1:1:133–34.
13. Pritchard, "Dark Days," 4:8–9.

CHAPTER 5

1. R. J. Patterson, "Mrs. Abraham Lincoln," *Chicago Tribune*, Aug. 29, 1875, 16; Robert Lincoln to Elizabeth Edwards, Aug. 7, 1875, LB, 1:1:135; Robert Lincoln to Elizabeth Edwards, Chicago, Jan. 17, 1876, folder 1, box 2, IF; Lutz White, "Now and Then: Before the Tardy Bell Rings," *Aurora Beacon-News*, Jan. 1, 1933, 6. For an examination of Mary's suicide attempt, see Emerson, *The Madness of Mary Lincoln*, 67–70; Norbert Hirschhorn, "Mary Lincoln's 'Suicide Attempt': A Physician Reconsiders the Evidence," *Lincoln Herald* 104, no. 3 (fall 2003): 94–98.
2. Descriptions based on Bellevue Place Sanitarium advertising brochures, n.d., 2 pages, and 1895, 15 pages, Batavia Historical Society, Batavia, Illinois; "Mrs. Lincoln: A Visit to Her by 'The Post and Mail' Correspondent," *Chicago Post and Mail*, July 13, 1875; Ross, "Mary Todd Lincoln, Patient at Bellevue Place."
3. For example, see "Personal," *Chicago Tribune*, Aug. 22, 1875, 5, which declared Mary was partially restored to health and well enough to visit Elizabeth Edwards in Springfield, likely not to return to Bellevue Place.
4. "Patient Progress Reports for Bellevue Place," 52, 55, transcribed in Ross, "Mary Todd Lincoln, Patient at Bellevue Place," 32, 33; Dr. R. J. Patterson to Myra Bradwell, Batavia, Ill., Aug. 9, 1875, folder 23, box 2, IF; "Franc B. Wilkie," *Biographical Sketches of Leading Men of Chicago* (Chicago: Wilson & St. Clair, 1868), 580–81.
5. Alice D. Shipman, interview by Ida Tarbell, quoted in "Mary Todd Lincoln: Wife of Abraham Lincoln—Part 2," *Ladies' Home Journal* (Mar. 1928), 223; Mary Lincoln to Mrs. Paul R. Shipman, Leamington, England, Oct. 27, 1870, in Turner and Turner, *Mary Todd Lincoln*, 578–79; untitled article, *Quincy* [Ill.] *Whig*, Jan. 19, 1871, 2; "Adam Badeau's Letter," *Chicago Tribune*, Jan. 17, 1887, 10.
6. Keckley, *Behind the Scenes*, 130–31.
7. Elizabeth Edwards to Robert Lincoln, Springfield, Nov. 5, 1875, folder 16, box 2, IF.
8. Bellevue Place Sanitarium advertising brochures, n.d., 2 pages, and 1895, 15 pages, Batavia Historical Society, Batavia, Ill.; "Mrs. Lincoln," *Chicago Post and Mail*, July 13, 1875.
9. "Reason Restored: Mrs. Lincoln Will Soon Return from Her Brief Visit to the Insane Asylum," *Chicago Times*, Aug. 24, 1875, 4.
10. Untitled editorial, *Chicago Times*, Aug. 24, 1875, 4.
11. *Chicago Post and Mail*, Aug. 21, 1875, quoted in "Mrs. Lincoln: Startling Interview upon Her Case with Judge Bradwell," *Chicago Post and Mail*, Aug. 23, 1875, clipping, folder 31, box 2, IF.

12. Robert Lincoln to Dr. R. J. Patterson, Sept. 2, 1875, folder 3, box 2, IF; Dr. R. J. Patterson to Robert Lincoln, Batavia, Ill., Sept. 7, 1875, folder 23, box 2, IF; Elizabeth Edwards to Robert Lincoln, Springfield, Aug. 17, 1875, folder 16, box 2, IF.
13. "Mrs. Lincoln: Startling Interview upon Her Case with Judge Bradwell," *Chicago Post and Mail*, Aug. 23, 1875, clipping, folder 31, box 2, IF.
14. Dr. R. J. Patterson to Robert Lincoln, Batavia, Ill., Aug. 20, 1875, folder 23, box 2, IF; "Mrs. Lincoln," *Illinois State Journal*, Aug. 25, 1875, clipping, IF; "Mrs. Abraham Lincoln," *Boston Globe*, Aug. 25, 1875, 1; untitled article, *Chicago Tribune*, Aug. 28, 1875, 8.

CHAPTER 6

1. For an excellent sociological study of the growth of Abraham Lincoln's reputation from 1865 to 1909, see Barry Schwartz, *Abraham Lincoln and the Forge of National Memory* (Chicago: University of Chicago Press, 2000).
2. Robert Lincoln to Elizabeth Edwards, Aug. 7, 1875, LB, 1:1:133–39.
3. Robert Lincoln to Myra Bradwell, Chicago, Aug. 13, 1875, handwritten copy by Myra Bradwell, folder 1, cont. 8, part 2, RTLFP; also in folder 1, box 2, IF.
4. Elizabeth Edwards to Robert Lincoln, Aug. 13, 1875, folder 16, box 2, IF.
5. Robert Lincoln to Sally Orne, June 1, 1875, and to Ninian Edwards, Nov. 15, 1875, folder 2, box 2, IF, and to Elizabeth Edwards, Aug. 7, 1875, LB, 1:1:133–34.
6. Robert Lincoln to Myra Bradwell, Chicago, Aug. 14, 1875, photographic copy and handwritten copy by Myra Bradwell on *Chicago Legal News* letterhead, folder 1, cont. 8, part 2, RTLFP; also in folder 1, box 2, IF, and LB, 1:1:143–44. See also Richard Patterson to Myra Bradwell, Aug. 9, 1875, folder 23, box 2, IF; Robert Lincoln to Elizabeth Edwards, Aug. 10, 1875, LB, 1:1:141–42.
7. Elizabeth Edwards to Robert Lincoln, Springfield, Aug. 12, 1875, folder 16, box 2, IF.
8. Robert Lincoln to Mary Lincoln, Chicago, Aug. 15, 1875, handwritten copy by Myra Bradwell on *Chicago Legal News* letterhead, folder 1, cont. 8, part 2, RTLFP; also in folder 1, box 2, IF.
9. Emphasis in original. R. J. Patterson to J. B. Bradwell, Batavia, Aug. 18, 1875, photographic copy and handwritten copy by Myra Bradwell on *Chicago Legal News* letterhead, folder 1, cont. 8, part 2, RTLFP; also in folder 23, box 2, IF. Patterson's letter and Bradwell's response also in "Mrs. Abraham Lincoln: Correspondence of Dr. Patterson and Judge Bradwell," *Chicago Tribune*, Aug. 31, 1875, 8.
10. "Mrs. Abraham Lincoln: Correspondence of Dr. Patterson and Judge Bradwell," *Chicago Tribune*, Aug. 31, 1875, 8.
11. R. J. Patterson, "Mrs. Abraham Lincoln," *Chicago Tribune*, Aug. 29, 1875, 16.
12. Dr. R. J. Patterson to Robert Lincoln, Batavia, Ill., Sept. 7, 1875, folder 23, box 2, IF; Dr. Andrew McFarland to Robert Lincoln, Sept. 8, 1875, folder 20, box 2, IF.
13. "Mrs. Lincoln," *Chicago Tribune*, Sept. 12, 1875, 12. Dr. Andrew McFarland to Robert Lincoln, Sept. 10 and 11, 1875, folder 20, box 2, IF; Robert Lincoln to Dr. R. J. Patterson, Chicago, Sept. 9, 1875, LB, 1:1:147–48, and copy in folder 3, box 2, IF.

CHAPTER 7

1. Appointment of Robert T. Lincoln as Conservator for Estate of Mary Lincoln, June 14, 1875, Cook County Court Documents, folder 33, box 2, IF.
2. Elizabeth Edwards to Robert Lincoln, Nov. 5, 1875, folder 16, box 2, IF.

3. Robert Lincoln to David Davis, Nov. 16, 1875, and to Ninian Edwards, Dec. 21, 1875, folder 2, box 2, IF; and to Elizabeth Edwards, May 17, 1876, folder 3, box 2, IF.
4. Mary Lincoln to James Bradwell, Nov. 11, 1875, folder 2, box 1, IF.
5. Mary Lincoln to James Bradwell, Dec. 1, 1875, folder 2, box 1, and Ninian Edwards to Robert Lincoln, Springfield, Dec. 18, 1875, folder 17, box 2, IF.
6. Mary Lincoln to County Judge, Cook County, July 23, 1873, folder 2, box 1, IF; Envelope labeled "To be delivered to the County Judge of Cook Co.—upon death of Mrs. Abraham Lincoln," folder 35, box 2, IF; "Opening of a Letter Written by Mrs. Lincoln," *Chicago Tribune*, July 21, 1882, 8; "A Letter Left by Mrs. Lincoln," *New York Times*, July 23, 1882, 7.
7. Robert Lincoln, deposition on personal estate of Mary Lincoln, Sangamon County Court, Sept. 1882, and Robert Lincoln, Petition for Letters of Administration, and Bond of Administration, and Inventory of Real Estate, and Final Report of Administrator, Sangamon County Court, Sept. 1882, folder 2, cont. 8, part 2, RTLFP; also located in Mary Lincoln Estate File, Lincoln Collection, ALPL; "Mrs. Lincoln's Estate," *Washington Post*, Sept. 29, 1882, 1; "Estate of Mrs. Lincoln," *New York Times*, Sept. 29, 1882, 2.
8. Mary Todd Lincoln last will and testament, July 23, 1873, photographic copies of first and last pages in folder 1, cont. 8, part 2, RTLFP, summary in Pritchard, "Dark Days," 8:4–5.
9. Florence Snow to Rosemary Ketchum, July 1939, published in Snow, *Pictures on My Wall: A Lifetime in Kansas* (Lawrence: University of Kansas Press, 1945), 67.
10. Robert Lincoln, Final Report of Administrator, Sangamon County Court, Nov. 1884, Mary Lincoln Estate File, Lincoln Collection, ALPL.
11. Turner and Turner, *Mary Todd Lincoln*, 620, n. 5; and Mary Lincoln to Jacob Bunn, Pau, France, Oct. 23, 1876, and Jan. 31, 1877, ibid, 620–21, 623–24; "Mrs. Lincoln: She Corrects Some Reports Concerning Her Financial Condition," *Illinois State Journal*, Nov. 29, 1881, 1; Robert Lincoln to Jacob Bunn, Dec. 9, 1880, and to Edward L. Baker, Dec. 14, 1880, LB, 3:5:766, 767–68.
12. Ninian Edwards to Robert Lincoln, Springfield, Dec. 22, 1875, folder 17, box 2, IF; Robert Lincoln to Mary Lincoln, Chicago, Feb. 7, 1876, folder 3, box 2, IF, and LB, 1:1:162–64; Elizabeth Edwards to Robert Lincoln, Springfield, Feb. 9, 1876, folder 16, box 2, and Robert Lincoln to Elizabeth Edwards, Feb. 12, 1876, folder 3, box 2, IF.
13. Robert Lincoln to Judge M. R. M. Wallace, Dec. 10 and 15, 1875, folder 33, box 2, IF, and pp. 42–43, 45–46, vol. 47, William E. Barton Scrapbook, University of Chicago Library.
14. Ninian Edwards to Robert Lincoln, Springfield, Jan. 14, 1876, folder 17, box 2, IF; Elizabeth Edwards to Robert Lincoln, Springfield, Jan. 16, 1876, folder 16, box 2, IF; Robert Lincoln to Ninian Edwards, Chicago, Jan. 17, 1876, and Apr. 24 and Apr. 25, 1876, LB, 4:3:379–81, 415–16, 418–19; Robert Lincoln to Elizabeth Edwards, May 17, 1876, folder 3, box 2, IF, and LB, 1:1:168–69.
15. Verdict of the jury in the case of Mary Lincoln, June 15, 1876, folder 33, box 2, IF; copies, pp. 36 and 48, vol. 47, William E. Barton Scrapbook, University of Chicago Library; "A Happy Denouement: Mrs. Abraham Lincoln Restored to Her Reason and Freedom," *Chicago Times*, June 16, 1876, 3; "Mrs. President Lincoln: Her Restoration to Reason and Property," *Chicago Tribune*, June 16, 1876, 8; "Mrs. Lincoln," *Illinois State Journal*, June 16, 1876, 1; untitled article, *Chicago Times*, June 16, 1876, 4; "Mrs. Abraham Lincoln," *Chicago Legal News*, 8, no. 39 (June 17, 1876), 309.

16. Mary Lincoln petition to Cook County Court, June 1876, folder 33, box 2, IF; copies, pp. 36 and 48, vol. 47, William E. Barton Scrapbook, University of Chicago Library.
17. Mason Brayman, *Revised Statutes of the State of Illinois* (Springfield, Ill.: Walters & Weber Printers, 1845), 277; Ninian Edwards to Robert Lincoln, Springfield, Ill., June 17, 1876, Folder 17, Box 2, IF.
18. Verdict of the jury in the case of Mary Lincoln, June 15, 1876, folder 33, box 2, IF; copies, pp. 36 and 48, vol. 47, William E. Barton Scrapbook, University of Chicago.
19. Conservator of Mary Lincoln, Account of Receipts and Disbursements, June 15, 1876, folders 30 and 33, box 2, IF.
20. Leonard Swett to David Davis, Chicago, May 24, 1875, folder A-73, box 5, David Davis Family Papers, ALPL; "Clouded Reason," *Chicago Tribune*, May 20, 1875, 1; "Mrs. Lincoln," *Chicago Inter Ocean*, May 20, 1875, 1.

CHAPTER 8

1. Robert Lincoln to Elizabeth Edwards, Aug. 7, 1875, LB, 1:1:138; Elizabeth Edwards to Robert Lincoln, Springfield, Sept. 22, 1875, folder 16, box 2, IF.
2. "Mrs. Abraham Lincoln," *Chicago Legal News* 8, no. 39 (June 17, 1876): 309.
3. Ninian Edwards to Robert Lincoln, Springfield, Ill., June 17, 1876, folder 17, box 2, IF.
4. Ninian Edwards to Robert Lincoln, June 17, 1876, folder 71, box 2, IF.
5. Robert Lincoln to David Davis, Sept. 21 and Nov. 9, 1871, folder A-109, box 7, David Davis Family Papers, ALPL; Mary Lincoln to David Davis, Nov. 9, 1871, Turner and Turner, *Mary Todd Lincoln*, 597–98.
6. Mary Lincoln to Leonard Swett, Jan. 12 and Feb. [n.d.], 1867, Turner and Turner, *Mary Todd Lincoln*, 405–6, 408–9.
7. Leonard Swett to David Davis, May 24, 1875, folder A-73, box 5, David Davis Family Papers, ALPL.
8. Emphasis in original. Mary Lincoln to Myra Bradwell, Springfield, Ill., June 18, 1876, photographic copies of first four pages of letter and copy of complete letter in Myra Pritchard's handwriting, folder 2, cont. 8, part 2, RTLFP.
9. William Herndon to Jesse Weik, Springfield, Ill., Jan. 8, 1886, in Hertz, *Hidden Lincoln*, 128–29.
10. Abraham Lincoln to Joshua Speed, Oct. 22, 1846, Roy P. Basler, ed., Marion Dolores Pratt and Lloyd A. Dunlap, asst. eds., *The Collected Works of Abraham Lincoln*, 8 vols. (New Brunswick, N.J.: Rutgers University Press, 1953–55), 1:391; Ida M. Tarbell, *In the Footsteps of the Lincolns* (New York: Harper, 1924), 253.
11. Ninian Edwards to Leonard Swett, Springfield, Ill., June 22 and June 24, 1876, and to Robert Lincoln, Springfield, Ill., June 26, 1876, folder 17, box 2, IF; Jacob Bunn to Robert Lincoln, June 24, 1876, folder 11, box 2, IF; Mary Lincoln to Jacob Bunn, Pau, France, Jan. 31, 1877, Turner and Turner, *Mary Todd Lincoln*, 623–24; Robert Lincoln to Jacob Bunn, Dec. 9, 1880, and to Edward L. Baker, Dec. 14, 1880, LB, 5:3:766, 767–68.
12. Emphasis in original. Mary Lincoln to James Bradwell, Springfield, Ill., June 22, 1876, copy of letter in Myra Pritchard's handwriting, folder 2, cont. 8, part 2, RTLFP.
13. Emphasis in original. Mary Lincoln to Robert Lincoln, June 19, 1876, Turner and Turner, *Mary Todd Lincoln*, 615–16.
14. Ninian Edwards to Leonard Swett, Springfield, June 22 and 24, 1876, folder 17, box 2, IF; Leonard Swett to Ninian Edwards, June 20, 1876, folder 27, box 2, IF, and July 1, 1876, LB, 1:1:172–79.

15. Thomas F. Schwartz, "'My stay on Earth, is growing very short': Mary Todd Lincoln's Letters to Willis Danforth and Elizabeth Swing," *Journal of Illinois History* 6 (summer 2003): 125–36; "Mrs. Abraham Lincoln: What Her Pastor, Prof. Swing, Says about Her Insanity," *Chicago Times*, Aug. 29, 1875, 1; untitled article, *Chicago Times*, Aug. 30, 1875, 4.
16. Emphasis in original. Mary Lincoln to Myra Bradwell, Springfield, Ill., July 7, 1876, copy of letter in Myra Pritchard's handwriting, folder 2, cont. 8, part 2, RTLFP.
17. Emphasis in original. Mary Lincoln to Myra Bradwell, Springfield, Ill., July 14, 1876, Pritchard, "Dark Days," 8:10–11.

CHAPTER 9

1. Helm, *True Story of Mary*, 298.
2. Mary Lincoln to Edward Lewis Baker Jr., Pau, France, June 22, 1879, Turner and Turner, *Mary Todd Lincoln*, 682.
3. Elizabeth Edwards to Robert Lincoln, Oct. 29, 1876, folder 16, box 2, IF.
4. Emphasis in original. Mary Lincoln to Mary Harlan Lincoln, Frankfort, Mar. 22, 1869, Turner and Turner, *Mary Todd Lincoln*, 506.
5. See Mary Lincoln to Jacob Bunn, Dec. 12, 1876, Turner and Turner, *Mary Todd Lincoln*, 622.
6. Emphasis in original. Mary Lincoln to Myra Bradwell, Pau, France, Dec. 1, 1876, Pritchard, "Dark Days," 9:1–4.
7. Emphasis in original. Mary Lincoln to Myra Bradwell, Pau, France, Apr. 12, 1877, Pritchard, "Dark Days," 9:4–6.
8. See Turner and Turner, *Mary Todd Lincoln*, 665–67.
9. Emphasis in original. Mary Lincoln to Jacob Bunn, Naples, Apr. 29, 1878, Turner and Turner, *Mary Todd Lincoln*, 666–67.
10. "Personalities," *Cincinnati Commercial*, Mar. 6, 1878, 4, reprinted from *New York Star*; "Mrs. Lincoln's Present Residence," *New York Times*, Apr. 6, 1878, 5.
11. John Addington Symonds, *New and Old: A Volume of Verse* (London: Smith, Edler, & Co., 1880), 167–169.
12. Emphasis in original. Mary Lincoln to Myra Bradwell, Sorrento, Italy, Apr. 22, 1878, photographic copy of first page of letter in folder 2, cont. 8, part 2, RTLFP, entire letter in Pritchard, "Dark Days," 9:7–10.
13. "Departures for Europe," *New York Times*, June 13, 1878; "Marine Intelligence," *New York Times*, June 23, 1878.
14. Emphasis in original. Mary Lincoln to Myra Bradwell, Pau, France, July 4, 1878, Pritchard, "Dark Days," 9:10–12.
15. Emphasis in original. Mary Lincoln to Myra Bradwell, Pau, France, July 6, 1878, Pritchard, "Dark Days," 9:12–13.
16. "The Merry City," *Chicago Tribune*, Aug. 18, 1878, 11.
17. "Passengers Arrived," *New York Times*, Oct. 12, 1879. This notice reports Myra Bradwell arriving from Liverpool, England, on the steamship *Montreal*.
18. Emphasis in original. Mary Lincoln to Myra Bradwell, Pau, France, July 19, 1878, Pritchard, "Dark Days," 9:13–14.
19. "Mrs. Lincoln's Illness," *New York Times*, Oct. 31, 1880, 5; "Mrs. Lincoln in Want," *New York Times*, Nov. 23, 1881, 5; Helm, *True Story of Mary*, 298–99; Mary Lincoln to Edward Lewis Baker, Pau, France, Jan. 19 and June 12, 1880, Turner and Turner, *Mary Todd Lincoln*, 695, 699.

20. "Sarah Bernhardt Beset," *The* [New York] *Sun*, Oct. 28, 1880, 3.
21. Sarah Bernhardt, *My Double Life: Memoirs of Sarah Bernhardt* (London: William Heinemann, 1907), 354.
22. Affidavit of Decease, Mary Lincoln Estate File, Lincoln Collection, ALPL; "Mary Todd Lincoln: Her Death in This City at 8 o'Clock Sunday Evening," *Illinois State Journal*, July 17, 1882, 6; "Death of Mrs. Lincoln," *New York Times*, July 17, 1882, 1; "Obituary: Death at Springfield, Illinois, of the Widow of Abraham Lincoln," *Chicago Tribune*, July 17, 1882, 2; Thomas W. Dresser to Jesse Weik, Springfield, Ill., Jan. 3, 1889, Wilson and Davis, *Herndon's Informants*, 671; Evans, *Mrs. Abraham Lincoln*, 344; Hirschhorn and Feldman, "Mary Lincoln's Final Illness," 536. "Laid to Rest: The Last Sad Rites Paid to the Remains of Mary Todd Lincoln," *Illinois State Journal*, July 20, 1882, 1; "Dust to Dust: The Body of Mrs. Abraham Lincoln Consigned to the Tomb," *Chicago Tribune*, July 20, 1882, 7.

EDITOR'S EPILOGUE

1. Mary Lincoln to Robert Lincoln, June 19, 1876, Turner and Turner, *Mary Todd Lincoln*, 615–16.
2. Robert Lincoln to Rev. Henry Darling, Nov. 15, 1877, folder 38, box 6, Lincoln Collection, Miscellaneous Manuscripts, Department of Special Collections, University of Chicago Library.
3. Robert Lincoln to Elizabeth Edwards, Apr. 18, 1879, Robert Todd Lincoln Papers, Allen County Public Library, Fort Wayne, Ind.
4. Ibid.
5. Historians W. A. Evans and Carl Sandburg began the Mamie story in separate 1932 biographies, both without citation. Sandburg's account was especially egregious, however, as he claimed Robert's entire family went to Springfield to see Mary. The newspaper accounts and Robert's letters prove this untrue. In 1953 Ruth Painter Randall, who cited Evans, repeated the Mamie story, and it has been considered authentic by subsequent historians. Untitled article, *Illinois State Journal*, May 27, 1881, 6, and May 28, 1881, 4, 6; Robert Lincoln to George C. Clark, May 23, 1881, and to General O. O. Howard, June 2, 1881, and to Benjamin Richardson, June 3, 1881, and to George J. Hagar, June 3, 1881, LB, 6:4:344–45, 365, 374, 376–77; Robert Lincoln to Sally Orne, June 2, 1881, Robert Todd Lincoln Papers, ALPL; Evans, *Mrs. Abraham Lincoln*, 53; Carl Sandburg and Paul M. Angle, *Mary Lincoln, Wife and Widow* (New York: Harcourt, Brace, 1932), 158; Randall, *Mary Lincoln*, 440.
6. Cyrus West Field was an American businessman and financier who led the Atlantic Telegraph Company, the company that successfully laid the first telegraph cable across the Atlantic Ocean in 1858. He had previously raised more than three hundred thousand dollars in public subscriptions for Mrs. Garfield. His brother, Stephen Field, was appointed to the U.S. Supreme Court in 1863 by Mary's husband, President Abraham Lincoln. "Mrs. Lincoln in Want," *New York Times*, Nov. 22, 1881, 5; "Mrs. Lincoln: Broad Denial of the Stories Set Afloat by Dr. Sayre," *Chicago Tribune*, Nov. 24, 1881, 3.
7. "Mrs. Lincoln in Want," *New York Times*, Nov. 22, 1881, 5.
8. Springer was a Democrat from Springfield, Ill. The other three physicians were neurologist Meredith Clymer, ophthalmologist Hermann Knapp, and surgeon William Pancoast. "New York: The Health of Mrs. Abraham Lincoln Not Improving: Examination of Her Condition by Several Distinguished Physicians," *Chicago Tribune*, Jan.

15, 1882, 6; Mary Lincoln to Noyes W. Miner, Jan. 3, 1882, Turner and Turner, *Mary Todd Lincoln*, 711; "William McKendree Springer," entry in *Biographical Directory of the United States Congress*, accessible online at http://bioguide.congress.gov/scripts/biodisplay.pl?index=S000757 (accessed March 18, 2010).

9. *Congressional Record*, 47th Cong. 1st sess., 1882, 13:402; "New York: The Health of Mrs. Abraham Lincoln Not Improving," *Chicago Tribune*, Jan. 15, 1882, 6.
10. *Congressional Record*, 47th Cong. 1st sess., 1882, 13:578, 652, 705–6, 882; "Mrs. Lincoln's Needs: The Relief Bill Passed by the Senate," *New York Times*, Jan. 25, 1882, 3; "Core's Bill," *Chicago Tribune*, Feb. 3, 1882, 2; "Mrs. Lincoln's Pension," *New York Times*, Mar. 17, 1882, 5.
11. Another contributing factor was her eye trouble, which pained her in bright light. "Mrs. Lincoln's Illness," *New York Times*, Oct. 31, 1880, 5; "Mrs. Lincoln's Health," *New York Times*, July 22, 1881, 3; Thomas W. Dresser to Jesse Weik, Jan. 3, 1889, Wilson and Davis, *Herndon's Informants*, 671.
12. Mary Edwards Brown, interview by Dorothy Meserve Kunhardt, published in "An Old Lady's Lincoln Memories," *Life*, Feb. 9, 1959, 57; J.C.A., "Mrs. Abraham Lincoln," *Chicago Tribune*, Aug. 6, 1881, 6.
13. Mary Edwards Brown, interview by Dorothy Meserve Kunhardt, "An Old Lady's Lincoln Memories," 57; Thomas W. Dresser to Jesse Weik, Jan. 3, 1889, Wilson and Davis, *Herndon's Informants*, 671; "Mrs. Lincoln's Health," *New York Times*, July 22, 1881, 3.
14. Mary Edwards Brown, interview by Dorothy Meserve Kunhardt, "An Old Lady's Lincoln Memories," 57.
15. Mary L. D. Putnam to her sons St. Clair and Clement Putnam, Dec. 8, 1882, extract sent from Paul Angle to William E. Barton, Jan. 10, 1927, William Barton Scrapbook, vol. 63, Lincoln Collection, University of Chicago Library.
16. J.C.A., "Mrs. Abraham Lincoln," *Chicago Tribune*, Aug. 6, 1881, 6.
17. "Mrs. Lincoln's Distress," *Chicago Tribune*, Oct. 2, 1881, 2; "Mrs. Lincoln Going to Canada," *New York Times*, Oct. 10, 1881, 4.
18. "I wish my remains to be clothed in the white silk dress, which will be found in the lower drawer of the bureau in my room. I desire that my body, shall remain for two days (48) hours, without the lid of the coffin being screwed down. On the 3rd day, after my death, Professor Swing, acceding, I wish the coffin taken to the latter's church, he preaching the funeral sermon from the 23d Psalm. 'Yea, though I walk through the valley of the shadow of death, I will fear no evil: for thou art with me; thy rod and thy staff they comfort me.' My coffin I wish to be of solid rosewood, plain, but massive silver plate with this inscription.

    'Mary Lincoln
    Died ——
    "He, giveth his beloved sleep"

    On the *fourth*, 4th day after my decease, I wish my remains placed beside my dear husband and Taddies' on one side of me." Mary Lincoln to Robert Lincoln, Aug. 1874, Lincoln Collection, ALPL, published in Schwartz, "My Stay on Earth Is Growing Very Short," 130.
19. Charles Sweet (for Robert T. Lincoln) to Mrs. Ninian Edwards, Oct. 26, 1882, and Charles Sweet (for Robert T. Lincoln) to Mrs. John Baker, Oct. 26, 1882, folder 34,

box 2, IF; Elizabeth Edwards to Robert Lincoln, Springfield, Nov. 9, 1882, folder 16, box 2, IF; Florence Snow to Rosemary Ketchum, July 1939, in Snow, *Pictures on My Wall*, 71–72. "You have been most lavish in your distribution of various articles, and the parties, who have shared the bounty, are truly grateful," Elizabeth Edwards wrote. "I wrote to your wife, while feeling nervous, and weary, and fear that I was not sufficiently enthusiastic in my praise, for her kind and laborious effort, in giving pleasure and comfort to so many, and to some, who are in depressed circumstances. It is a sad fact, that the young members of our several families, have been lamentably unsuccessful, and greatly embarrassed those who should not have been made uncomfortable."

20. "This examination was a business I might have done at any time after her death in 1882 but there was no reason for thinking it of consequence and I dreaded it," Robert wrote. Robert Lincoln to John Hay, Chicago, Nov. 19, 1895, reel 8, John Milton Hay Papers, John Hay Library, Brown University, Providence, R.I.
21. Robert Lincoln to Abram Wakeman, Nov. 28, 1908, LB, 41:71:430; Robert Lincoln to Le Grand Van Valkenburgh, May 26, 1913, Robert Todd Lincoln Papers, Lincoln Collection, ALPL; Robert Lincoln to Emily Todd Helm, June 15, 1913, Robert Todd Lincoln Papers, CHM.
22. Eleanor Gridley, "Presentation of Bronze Bust of Mrs. Myra Bradwell, First Woman Lawyer of Illinois," Transactions of the Illinois State Historical Society, publication no. 38 (May 1931): 6.

BIBLIOGRAPHY

ARCHIVES

Abraham Lincoln Presidential Library, Springfield, Illinois
  Abraham Lincoln Association Papers
  David Davis Family Papers
  Elizabeth Todd Grimsley Papers
  Henry Horner Lincoln Collection Papers
  Robert Todd Lincoln Papers
Allegheny College, Meadville, Pennsylvania
  Ida M. Tarbell–Lincoln Collection
Allen County Public Library, Fort Wayne, Indiana
  Mary Todd Lincoln Insanity File
  Robert Todd Lincoln Collection
Brown University, Providence, Rhode Island
  John Milton Hay Collection
Chicago History Museum, Chicago, Illinois
  Myra Pritchard Papers
  Robert Todd Lincoln Papers
Friends of Hildene, Inc., Manchester, Vermont
  Robert Todd Lincoln Collection
  John Goff Papers
Henry E. Huntington Library, San Marino, California
  Ward Hill Lamon Papers
Illinois Regional Archives Depository, University of Illinois at Springfield, Springfield, Illinois.
Library of Congress, Washington, D.C.
  Albert J. Beveridge Papers
  Herndon-Weik Collection of Lincolniana
  Robert Todd Lincoln Family Papers
  David C. Mearns Papers
  Randall [James G. and Ruth Painter] Family Papers
Myra Pritchard Family Papers, privately owned
University of Chicago, Joseph Regenstein Library, Chicago, Illinois
  William E. Barton Collection
  Lincoln Miscellaneous Manuscripts
University of Kentucky, Special Collections and Digital Programs, King Library
  William Townsend Papers

NEWSPAPERS

Aurora [Ill.] *Beacon-News*
Batavia [Ill.] *Herald*
Boston Globe
Chicago Tribune
Chicago Inter Ocean
Chicago Times
Chicago Post and Mail
Chicago Journal
Chicago Morning Courier
Cincinnati Commercial
Illinois State Journal
Illinois State Register
New York Times
The [New York] *Sun*
Quincy [Ill.] *Whig*
Washington Post

BOOKS

Baker, Jean H. *Mary Todd Lincoln: A Biography*. New York: W. W. Norton, 1987.

Barton, William E. *The Life of Abraham Lincoln*. 2 vols. Indianapolis: Bobbs-Merrill, 1925.

———. *The Women Lincoln Loved*. Indianapolis: Bobbs-Merrill, 1927.

Basler, Roy P., ed., Marion Dolores Pratt and Lloyd A. Dunlap, asst. eds. *The Collected Works of Abraham Lincoln*. 9 vols. New Brunswick, N.J.: Rutgers University Press, 1953–55.

Bayne, Julia Taft. *Tad Lincoln's Father*. 1931. Reprint, Lincoln: University of Nebraska Press, 2001.

Bernhardt, Sarah. *My Double Life: Memoirs of Sarah Bernhardt*. London: William Heinemann, 1907.

Berry, Stephen. *House of Abraham: Lincoln and the Todds, a Family Divided by War*. Boston: Houghton Mifflin, 2007.

Biographical Directory of the United States Congress. Accessible online at http://bioguide.congress.gov/scripts/biodisplay.pl?index=S000757.

Biographical Sketches of the Leading Men of Chicago. Chicago: Wilson & St. Clair Publishers, 1868.

Boyden, Anna L. *War Reminiscences, or Echoes from Hospital and White House*. Boston: D. Lathrop and Company, 1887.

Brayman, Mason. *Revised Statutes of the State of Illinois*. Springfield, Ill.: Walters & Weber Printers, 1845.

Brooks, Noah. *Washington in Lincoln's Time*, Herbert Mitgang, ed. New York: Rinehart & Company, 1958.

Bullard, F. Lauristan. *Tad and His* Father. Boston: Little, Brown, 1917.

Burlingame, Michael, ed. *An Oral History of Abraham Lincoln: John G. Nicolay's Interviews and Essays*. Carbondale: Southern Illinois University Press, 1996.

Donald, David. *Lincoln's Herndon*. New York: Alfred A. Knopf, 1948.

———. *Lincoln Reconsidered*. New York: Alfred A. Knopf, 1956; repr. New York: Vintage Books, 2001.

Emerson, Jason. *The Madness of Mary Lincoln*. Carbondale: Southern Illinois University Press, 2007.
Evans, W. A. *Mrs. Abraham Lincoln: A Study of Her Personality and Her Influence on Abraham Lincoln*. New York: Alfred A. Knopf, 1932.
Friedman, Jane M. *America's First Woman Lawyer: The Biography of Myra Bradwell*. Buffalo, N.Y.: Prometheus Books, 1993.
Gridley, Eleanor. *The Story of Abraham Lincoln, or The Journey from the Log Cabin to the White House*. New York: Eaton & Mains, 1900.
Helm, Katherine. *The True Story of Mary, Wife of Lincoln*. New York: Harper and Brothers, 1928.
Herndon, William H., and Jesse W. Weik. *Herndon's Lincoln*. Douglas L. Wilson and Rodney O. Davis, eds. 1889. Reprint, Urbana: University of Illinois Press, 2006.
Hertz, Emanuel. *The Hidden Lincoln: From the Letters and Papers of William H. Herndon*. New York: Viking Press, 1938.
Hickey, James T. *The Collected Writings of James T. Hickey from Publications of the Illinois State Historical Society, 1953–1984*. Springfield: Illinois State Historical Society, 1990.
History of Sangamon County, Illinois. Chicago: Interstate Publishing, 1881.
Hodgen, Godfrey. *Woodrow Wilson's Right Hand: The Life of Col. Edward M. House*. New Haven: Yale University Press, 2006.
Keckley, Elizabeth. *Behind the Scenes: Thirty Years a Slave and Four Years in the White House*. 1868. Reprint, New York: Arno Press, 1968.
King, Willard L. *Lincoln's Manager: David Davis*. Cambridge: Harvard University Press, 1960.
Mearns, David C. *The Lincoln Papers: The Story of the Collection with Selections to July 4, 1861*. 2 vols. Garden City, N.Y.: Doubleday and Company, Inc., 1948.
Morrow, Honoré Willsie. *Mary Todd Lincoln: An Appreciation of the Wife of Abraham Lincoln*. New York.: William Morrow & Company, 1928.
Neely, Mark E., and R. Gerald McMurtry. *The Insanity File: The Case of Mary Todd Lincoln*. Carbondale: Southern Illinois University Press, 1986.
Past and Present of Kane County, Illinois. Chicago: W. Le Baron Jr. & Co., 1878.
Pratt, Harry E. The *Personal Finances of Abraham Lincoln*. Springfield, Ill.: Abraham Lincoln Association, 1943.
Randall, Ruth Painter. *Mary Lincoln: Biography of a Marriage*. Boston: Little, Brown & Company, 1953.
Sandburg, Carl. *The Lincoln Collector: The Story of the Oliver R. Barrett Lincoln Collection*. New York: Bonanza Books, 1960.
Sandburg, Carl, and Paul M. Angle. *Mary Lincoln: Wife and Widow*. New York: Harcourt, Brace and Company, 1932.
Schwartz, Barry. *Abraham Lincoln and the Forge of National Memory*. Chicago: University of Chicago Press, 2000.
Snow, Florence. *Pictures on My Wall: A Lifetime in Kansas*. Lawrence: University of Kansas Press, 1945.
Sotos, John G. *The Physical Lincoln Sourcebook*. Printing 1.1a. Mt. Vernon, Va.: Mt. Vernon Book Systems, 2008.
Stoddard, William O. *Inside the White House in War Times*. Michael Burlingame, ed. 1890. Reprint, Lincoln: University of Nebraska Press, 2000.
Swisshelm, Jane Grey. *Half a Century*. Chicago: Jansen, McClurg & Company, 1880.

Symonds, John Addington. *New and Old: A Volume of Verse.* London: Smith, Edler, & Co., 1880.

Tarbell, Ida M. *The Life of Abraham Lincoln.* 2 vols. New York: Lincoln Memorial Association, 1900.

———. *Father Abraham.* New York: Moffat, Yard, 1909.

———. *In the Footsteps of the Lincolns.* New York: Harper & Brothers, 1924.

———. *All in the Day's Work.* New York: Macmillan Company, 1939.

Townsend, William H. *Lincoln and His Wife's Home Town.* Indianapolis: Bobbs-Merrill, 1929.

Turner, Justin G., and Linda Levitt Turner. *Mary Todd Lincoln: Her Life and Letters.* New York: Alfred A. Knopf, 1972.

U.S. Congress. *Congressional Globe.* 40th Congress, 3rd sess., 1869. Vol. 2.

———. *Congressional Globe.* 41st Cong., 2nd sess., 1870. Vol. 6.

———. *Congressional Record.* 47th Cong., 1st sess., 1882. Vol. 13.

Verneuil, Louis. *The Fabulous Life of Sarah Bernhardt.* Ernest Boyd, trans. New York: Harper & Brothers Publishers, 1942.

Wilson, Douglas L. *Honor's Voice: The Transformation of Abraham Lincoln.* New York: Alfred A. Knopf, 1998.

Wilson, Douglas L., and Rodney O. Davis, eds. *Herndon's Informants: Letters, Interviews, and Statements about Abraham Lincoln.* Urbana: University of Illinois Press, 1998.

Woman's Who's Who in America. New York: American Commonwealth Company, 1914.

ARTICLES

Bach, Jennifer L. "Was Mary Todd Lincoln Bipolar?" *Journal of Illinois History* 8, no. 4 (winter 2005): 281–94.

Basler, Roy P. "The Authorship of the 'Rebecca' Letters." *Abraham Lincoln Quarterly* 2, no. 2 (June 1942): 80–90.

Brussel, James A. "Mary Todd Lincoln: A Psychiatric Study." *Psychiatric Quarterly* 15, supp. 1 (January 1941): 7–26.

Bullard, F. Lauriston. "Mrs. Lincoln's Pension." *Lincoln Herald* 49 no. 2 (June 1947): 22–27.

Burlingame, Michael. "'A Hard-Hearted Conscious Liar and an Oily Hypocrite': Henry B. Rankin's Reliability as a Lincoln Informant." In Jesse W. Weik, *The Real Lincoln: A Portrait,* Michael Burlingame, ed., 389–98. Lincoln: University of Nebraska Press, 2003. Book originally published 1922.

Emerson, Jason. "New Mary Lincoln Letter Found." *Journal of the Illinois State Historical Society,* 101, nos. 3, 4 (fall-winter 2008): 315–28.

Gilliam, Nancy T. "A Professional Pioneer: Myra Bradwell's Fight to Practice Law." *Law and History Review* 5, no. 1 (spring 1987): 105–33.

Gridley, Eleanor. "Presentation of Bronze Bust of Mrs. Myra Bradwell, First Woman Lawyer of Illinois." Transactions of the Illinois State Historical Society. Publication no. 38 (May 1931): 6.

Hirschhorn, Norbert. "Mary Lincoln's 'Suicide Attempt': A Physician Reconsiders the Evidence." *Lincoln Herald* 104, no. 3 (fall 2003): 94–98.

Hirschhorn, Norbert, and Robert G. Feldman. "Mary Lincoln's Final Illness: A Medical and Historical Reappraisal." *Journal of the History of Medicine and Allied Sciences* 54, no. 4 (October 1999): 511–42.

Kunhardt, Dorothy Meserve. "An Old Lady's Lincoln Memories." *Life* 46, no. 6 (February 9, 1959): 57, 59–60.

"Mrs. Abraham Lincoln." *Chicago Legal News* 8, no. 39 (June 17, 1876): 309.

Neely, Mark E. "Abraham Lincoln did NOT Defend His Wife before the Committee on the Conduct of the War." *Lincoln Lore*, no. 1643, January 1975.

———. "Thurlow Weed, The New York Custom House, and Mrs. Lincoln's 'Treason.'" *Lincoln Lore*, no. 1679, January 1978.

Porter, Doris Replogle. "The Mysterious Browning Letter." *Lincoln Herald* 90, no. 1 (spring 1988): 20–23.

Rice, Judith A. "Ida M. Tarbell: A Progressive Look at Lincoln." *Journal of the Abraham Lincoln Association* 19, no. 1 (winter 1998): 57–72.

Robinson, Lelia J. "Women Lawyers in the United States." *Green Bag* 2, no. 1 (January 1890): 14.

Ross, Rodney A. "Mary Todd Lincoln: Patient at Bellevue Place, Batavia." *Journal of the Illinois State Historical Society* 63, no. 1 (spring 1970): 5–34.

Schwartz, Thomas F. "'My stay on Earth, is growing very short': Mary Todd Lincoln's Letters to Willis Danforth and Elizabeth Swing." *Journal of Illinois History* 6 (summer 2003): 125–36.

Shutes, Milton. "Mortality of the Five Lincoln Boys." *Lincoln Herald* 57, nos. 1. 2 (spring-summer 1955): 7.

"Some Intimate Glimpses into the Private Lives of the Members of the Robert Lincoln Family," *Lincoln Lore*, no. 1525, March1965.

Suarez, John M. "Mary Todd Lincoln: A Case Study." *American Journal of Psychiatry* 122, no. 7 (January 1966): 816–19.

Tarbell, Ida. "Mary Todd Lincoln: Wife of Abraham Lincoln—Part 2." *Ladies' Home Journal* (March 1928), 30–31, 218, 221, 223.

Warren, Louis A. "Mrs. Lincoln and 'Your Soldier Boy.'" *Lincoln Lore*, no. 683, May 11, 1942.

Wilson, Douglas L. "Abraham Lincoln and 'That Fatal First of January,'" *Civil War History*, 38, no. 2 (June 1992): 101–30.

———. "William H. Herndon and Mary Todd Lincoln." *Journal of the Abraham Lincoln Association* 22 (summer 2001): 1–26.

INDEX

Myra Helmer Pritchard was a champion golfer and tennis player and an amateur historian. She lived in Battle Creek, Michigan, with her husband, Dr. Stuart Pritchard, the president and general director of the W. K. Kellogg Foundation. Mrs. Pritchard was the owner of numerous heirlooms of the Abraham Lincoln family, which she inherited from her grandmother, Myra Bradwell, who was a close friend of Mary Todd Lincoln. Mrs. Pritchard died in 1947.

Jason Emerson is an award-winning historian and journalist who has been researching and writing about the Lincoln family for more than twenty-five years. His works include *The Madness of Mary Lincoln*, *Giant in the Shadows: The Life of Robert T. Lincoln*, and *Lincoln the Inventor*.

